T0339550

Cambridge Elements ≡

Elements in Historical Theory and Practice
edited by
Daniel Woolf
Queen's University, Ontario

HISTORIANS' VIRTUES

From Antiquity to the Twenty-First Century

Herman Paul
Leiden University

CAMBRIDGE
UNIVERSITY PRESS

Shaftesbury Road, Cambridge CB2 8EA, United Kingdom

One Liberty Plaza, 20th Floor, New York, NY 10006, USA

477 Williamstown Road, Port Melbourne, VIC 3207, Australia

314–321, 3rd Floor, Plot 3, Splendor Forum, Jasola District Centre,
New Delhi – 110025, India

103 Penang Road, #05–06/07, Visioncrest Commercial, Singapore 238467

Cambridge University Press is part of Cambridge University Press & Assessment,
a department of the University of Cambridge.

We share the University's mission to contribute to society through the pursuit of
education, learning and research at the highest international levels of excellence.

www.cambridge.org
Information on this title: www.cambridge.org/9781108994972

DOI: 10.1017/9781108993067

First published 2022

A catalogue record for this publication is available from the British Library.

ISBN 978-1-108-99497-2 Paperback
ISSN 2634-8616 (online)
ISSN 2634-8608 (print)

Historians' Virtues

From Antiquity to the Twenty-First Century

Elements in Historical Theory and Practice

DOI: 10.1017/9781108993067
First published online: September 2022

Herman Paul
Leiden University

Author for correspondence: Herman Paul, h.j.paul@hum.leidenuniv.nl

Abstract: Why do historians so often talk about objectivity, empathy, and fair-mindedness? What roles do such personal qualities play in historical studies? And why does it make sense to call them virtues rather than skills or habits? *Historians' Virtues* is the first publication to explore these questions in some depth. With case studies from across the centuries, this Element identifies major discontinuities in how and why historians talked about the marks of a good scholar. At the same time, it draws attention to long-term legacies that still exist today. Virtues were, and are, invoked in debates over the historian's task. They reveal how historians position themselves vis-à-vis political regimes, religious traditions, or neoliberal university systems. More importantly, they show that historical study not only requires knowledge and technical skills, but also makes demands on the character of its practitioners. This Element is also available as Open Access on Cambridge Core.

Keywords: scholarly virtues, scholarly vices, intellectual virtues, epistemic virtues, historiography

ISBNs: 9781108994972 (PB), 9781108993067 (OC)
ISSNs: 2634-8616 (online), 2634-8608 (print)

Contents

Introduction

Halfway through his widely used handbook, *The Pursuit of History* (7th ed., 2022), John Tosh devotes a couple of pages to what he calls 'the qualities of a historian'. He starts by quoting Samuel Johnson, who back in the eighteenth century dared to say that 'great abilities are not requisite for an historian', but proceeds to explain that this view is patently wrong. Among other things, historians must be critical. They must have an eye for detail and be able to abstract from particulars. In addition, they need a well-developed imagination and, if possible, a broad experience of life. In this context, Tosh cites another eighteenth-century luminary, Edward Gibbon, who described his short stint in parliament as ideal preparation for writing his great work *The History of the Decline and Fall of the Roman Empire* (6 vols., 1776–89): 'The eight sessions that I saw in parliament were a school of civil prudence, the first and most essential virtue of an historian.' Tosh agrees: he also believes that historians need to familiarize themselves with life outside the halls of academia to increase their 'ability to empathize with people in the past'.[1]

Historians' personal qualities also figure prominently in Tosh's chapter on source criticism. To grasp what a document does and does not say, or to understand to what uses it might be put, historians need 'ingenuity and flair' as well as a mind trained in what E. P. Thompson, writing in the 1970s, called 'a discipline of attentive disbelief'. Likewise, the historiographical parts of Tosh's book tell us about nineteenth-century historians who valued 'intuition', 'empathy', and 'sensitivity' or tried to be 'disinterested'.[2] And this is not yet all. Tosh's entire text is sprinkled with adjectives like 'careful', 'critical', 'conscientious', and 'meticulous', not to mention 'honest' and 'objective'. These adjectives qualify the way in which Tosh expects historians to work: not sloppily, but carefully; not naively, but critically. Indeed, they reveal that Tosh would like historians to possess a certain 'attitude of mind – an instinct almost'.[3] Like Gibbon in the eighteenth century and Thompson in the twentieth, Tosh tells his readers that historical scholarship requires personal qualities in its practitioners: carefulness, critical acumen, empathy, and ingenuity.

Trivial as they may seem, qualities of the kind that Tosh recommends are actually a source of contestation, not only among twenty–first century historians but across the centuries. Whenever scholars are dissatisfied with dominant ways of doing history, the marks of a good historian become the subject of discussion. Calls for revolution – against state-sponsored history writing, against male-dominated historiography, or against the strictures of a discipline that thwarts all experimentation – are typically supported by visionary images of what a good historian might look like. For instance, in the early 1950s, the Indian historian

---

[1] Tosh, *Pursuit*, 147, 148.   [2] Ibid., 154, 155, 162, 123.   [3] Ibid., 123.

Jadunath Sarkar spoke high-mindedly about historians' virtues in challenging an Indian tradition of historical writing that he saw as suffering from excessive nationalism and lack of interest in serious primary source research. 'We should intensify our industry', said Sarkar, 'sharpen our vigilance, and above all curb our natural tendency to self-glorification'. And again: 'We need above everything else that pure flame of the quest of truth, that fanatical devotion to our aim, regardless of fame or gain, which is the mark of the true scholar.' This was unadulterated virtue language, used in the service of a revolution against the so-called Poona School in Indian historiography.[4]

Hayden White, the medieval historian who turned into a harsh critic of the quasi-Rankean virtues applauded by Sarkar, serves as another example. His manifesto, 'The Burden of History' (1966), was one long objection to historians who pretended to be experts on the past on the basis of merely some 'general experience of human affairs, reading in peripheral fields, self-discipline, and *Sitzfleisch*'.[5] Inspired by modernist art and political radicalism alike, White's alternative demanded rather different qualities: the intellectual courage of a Jacob Burckhardt, the experimental attitude of a Norman O. Brown, and the moral earnestness of an Albert Camus.[6]

A little later, in the 1970s, feminist historians like Gerda Lerner also turned the spotlight on historians' personal qualities in rallying against 'the competitiveness which is structured into our institutional and professional life'. What Lerner dreamed of was a communal mode of doing scholarship, in which historians would be collaborators instead of competitors for status and resources. Over against the ills of academic careerism, Lerner therefore placed 'a new and as of yet untested model of supportive and engaged scholarship', which she believed would both reflect and shape the kind of persons that women's historians tried to become. In Lerner's view of things, then, women's history was not only an attempt to write women back into history, but also an experiment in practicing feminist virtues.[7] Echoes of this view can be heard in our day among advocates of 'slow scholarship' who argue that neoliberal university policies instil in scholars such bad habits as haste, sloppiness, and lack of collegiality, despite the fact that everyone knows, or should know, that patience, care, and attentiveness are among the marks of a true scholar.[8]

Apparently, historians' personal qualities – the subject of this Element – span the entire spectrum from Tosh to White or Lerner. They are taught to students in Historical Methods 101, but also staunchly debated in controversies over the aims of historical writing or the politics of university life. While some of these personal

---

[4] Sarkar, 'Progress', 36.   [5] White, 'Burden', 124.   [6] Ibid., 128, 129, 134.
[7] Lerner, *Majority*, vii, viii.
[8] For example, Karkov, *Slow Scholarship*; Simonsen, 'Consuming Time.'

qualities may seem self-evident (who would deny that historians must be careful?), they are also the stuff of endless debate, given that scholars only rarely agree on what is 'the first and most essential virtue of an historian' (Gibbon).

Insofar as historians of historiography have paid attention to such personal qualities, they have mostly done so in terms of 'virtues'. Basically, there are two reasons for this choice of terminology. First, as Gibbon's phrase already illustrated, eighteenth and nineteenth-century historians often classified the qualities needed for historical study as 'virtues'. They did so especially in educational contexts – telling their students in Tosh-like fashion that 'patience is the cardinal virtue of the scholar'[9] – and in reflections on the standards of their trade. Gibbonian formulas like the 'first' and 'highest virtue of an historian' enjoyed commonplace status in genres like the book review, the obituary, and the inaugural address.[10] Consequently, insofar as we are dealing with European historians in the time of Gibbon, Thomas Babington Macaulay, or Theodor Mommsen, we might use 'virtues' as an actors' category.

Most scholars, however, find this too limiting and prefer to use 'virtues' in a broader sense: not as an actors' category, but as an analytical term that can also be applied to periods and regions in which 'the first and most essential virtue of an historian' was an unfamiliar phrase.[11] Used as an analytical tool, the term conveys that personal qualities of the kind recommended by Tosh, ridiculed by White, and advocated by Lerner and the slow scholarship movement are no technical skills (like Latin reading proficiency) or cognitive abilities (like a good memory), but *traits of character.* Honesty, carefulness, conscientiousness, and the like are traits of character because they describe distinctive ways in which historians think, talk, teach, or write. These qualities are not occasional but habitual, ingrained in the personalities of their possessors, to the point of being almost second nature. Calling impartiality, meticulousness, or fairmindedness a virtue is therefore a way of highlighting that these are dispositions or character traits that scholars must possess to be good historians.[12]

Although this notion of virtue has a broadly Aristotelian ring to it, it is important to add that few scholars in the field try to draw sharp terminological distinctions. Even when they align themselves with philosophers or historians of science who speak more technically about 'epistemic virtues' (i.e., traits of character deemed necessary for the pursuit of epistemic goals such as knowledge and understanding),[13] historians of historiography typically prefer to keep

---

[9] Langlois and Seignobos, *Introduction*, 103.   [10] Paul, 'Ranke vs Schlosser', 37–40.

[11] See, for example, Meeus, 'Truth.'

[12] I elaborate on these conceptual distinctions in Paul, 'Scholarly Persona.'

[13] See Baehr, *Inquiring Mind*; Zagzebski, *Virtues of the Mind*.

their categories flexible and adaptable to different historical settings. Their purpose, after all, is not to *prescribe* what virtues historians should possess, but to *describe* what traits of character historians in a distant or more recent past expected each other to display. They want to know: Why did such qualities matter? What did it mean to be impartial, accurate, or critical? And why did historians so often disagree on the relative importance of these virtues?

One reason why historians' virtues have emerged on the agenda is that a cultural turn in the history of historiography has generated stimulating studies on historians' day-to-day work. While older literature often focussed on historians' methods or approaches, newer studies examine how historians tried to get access to archives, taught their students, reviewed each other's work, or remembered their deceased colleagues. Given that many of these studies focus on the era of Macaulay and Mommsen – a time in which 'virtue' was on everyone's lips – it is not surprising that they find historians caring a lot about virtues. Kasper Risbjerg Eskildsen, for instance, examines how seminar teaching in nineteenth-century Germany aimed to socialize students into virtues of criticism, adding that the main function of such virtues was to guarantee the credibility of historians' research.[14] Jo Tollebeek, likewise, argues that virtues like impartiality, accuracy, and thoroughness provided an emerging historical profession with a shared professional ethos.[15] More recently, Falko Schnicke has shown that this nineteenth-century ethos was so overwhelmingly masculine that it left little room for aspiring women historians.[16] In all these cases, virtues receive attention simply because scholars in the past saw them as important for research and teaching alike.

Others write about historians' virtues because they are interested in historicizing the 'moral economy' of modern-day scholarship (that is, the system of unwritten rules and expectations pertaining to how scholars do their work). Following Lorraine Daston and Peter Galison's pioneering book, *Objectivity* (2007),[17] several studies set out to trace the historical roots of concepts like impartiality, empathy, and sympathy.[18] Because most of these studies focus on a single virtue, they can trace how its meanings changed over time and examine how the virtue assumed different roles in different contexts. This not only allows for comparisons between historical studies and other fields but also shows that historians had no monopoly on qualities like impartiality. For this

---

[14] Eskildsen, 'Virtues'; Eskildsen, 'Inventing'; Eskildsen, 'Commentary.'
[15] Tollebeek, *Men of Character*; Tollebeek, 'Commemorative Practices.'
[16] Schnicke, *Männliche Disziplin*. See also Smith, *Gender of History*, and Garritzen, 'Pasha.'
[17] Daston and Galison, *Objectivity*.
[18] Murphy and Traninger, *Emergence of Impartiality*; Lanzioni, *Empathy*; Schliesser, *Sympathy*; Krajewski, von Schöning, and Wimmer, *Enzyklopädie der Genauigkeit*.

reason, it has been argued that virtues are a perfect prism for comparative historical research across the humanities or even between the sciences and the humanities.[19]

Finally, it is unmistakable that historians' virtues and, more broadly, their personae and professional identities also receive attention because these themes are resonating among academics today.[20] Whether or not they sympathize with the slow scholarship movement, many historians feel that twenty–first century academia puts a lot of pressure on precisely those virtues (carefulness, empathy, honesty) that Tosh presents as marks of a true historian. Also, in a world of big data, digital technologies, and declining prestige of the humanities, many historians wonder how their field will or should develop. Is Tosh's model of a conscientious archival researcher still viable in a funding system that privileges STEM disciplines over the arts or humanities? How much room is there for rebels à la White if academic survival chances depend on research assessment exercises? And does the looming prospect of climate disaster not call for other types of historians than those who consider historical study for purposes other than itself a breach of virtue? Seen from this perspective, historians' virtues are not an antiquarian topic: the theme touches on questions of professional identity that are as relevant today as they were in the eighteenth or nineteenth century.[21]

Despite this emerging interest in historians' virtues, a broad introductory survey of the theme does not yet exist. *Historians' Virtues* seeks to fill this lacuna. Targeted at graduate students and researchers new to the topic, this Element tries to explain why historians' personal qualities mattered in contexts as diverse as early Imperial China, seventeenth-century France, and post-World War II America. It presents a broad range of examples to illustrate the richness of the theme, while also addressing some more systematic questions: What are virtues? Why did historians care about such qualities, whether or not they actually called them 'virtues'? And why did historians throughout the centuries so often quarrel about virtues and their negative counterparts, the vices?

In addressing these questions, *Historians' Virtues* simultaneously draws and expands on an emerging body of literature.[22] On the one hand, this Element is much indebted to the scholarship of colleagues who in recent years have joined me in exploring the importance of virtues in historical studies. Some of their work will feature explicitly in the pages that follow. Also, this Element follows existing scholarship in adopting a broad working

---

[19] Engberts, *Scholarly Virtues*; Bod et al., 'Flow of Cognitive Goods'; Van Dongen and Paul, 'Introduction.'

[20] See, for example, Kivistö, *Vices of Learning*, vii.   [21] Paul, 'Sources', 147–50.

[22] In addition to the titles just mentioned, see Creyghton et al., 'Virtue Language'; Saarloos, 'Scholarly Self'; Domanska, 'Historians.'

definition of virtue. Following Rosalind Hursthouse and Glen Pettigrove, it understands a virtue to be 'an excellent trait of character. It is a disposition, well entrenched in its possessor ... to notice, expect, value, feel, desire, choose, act, and react in certain characteristic ways'.[23] As this definition is rather minimalist – it does not make any assumptions about 'the unity of the virtues' or the biological foundations of virtuous behaviour – it has the advantage of being widely applicable. It can capture a broad range of qualities that historians in different times and regions perceived as crucial for the pursuit of historical study.

On the other hand, this Element seeks to expand on existing scholarship in two significant ways. The first one is captured in its subtitle: 'From Antiquity to the twenty-first century.' Whereas most existing studies on historians' virtues focus on the nineteenth and twentieth centuries, this Element shows that these virtues have a centuries-long history. Given the current state of research, it is obviously impossible to offer anything close to a comprehensive account of how historians' virtues have developed over time. However, in the spirit of what David Armitage calls 'serial contextualization', it should be possible to present a limited but illustrative selection of case studies that exemplify how historians in different times thought about the virtues needed for historical study.[24] One of the advantages of such a broad temporal scope is that it enables us to see how much historians in the modern era were still indebted to centuries-old notions like the idea that historians' writings mirror their characters (*oratio speculum mentis*). Also, in showing that virtues like impartiality had roots far back in time, it helps explain why some of these qualities became heavily charged with historical connotations, to the point that some twentieth-century historians no longer saw a future for them.[25]

Secondly, unlike most existing studies, this book treats categories of virtue first and foremost as a *discourse*. Even if we equate virtues with character traits, the most remarkable thing about historians' virtues is that they were so widely discussed and disputed. Throughout the ages, scholars wrote passionately about virtues they considered important for historical studies. They spent many pages extolling Confucius as a model of virtue or criticizing Herodotus for his malicious attitudes. They quarrelled at length about the importance of impartiality or critical sense in an age of confessional rivalry. And when historical studies in nineteenth-century Europe turned into an academic discipline, professorial

---

[23] Hursthouse and Pettigrove, 'Virtue Ethics', § 1.1.   [24] Armitage, 'Big Idea', 498–9.

[25] Given that most existing scholarship focuses on Europe and North America – Ohara, 'Virtudes epistêmicas', Rogacz, 'Virtue', and Schulte Nordholt, 'African Historian' are still exceptions – it would be equally exciting to expand the geographical scope. This Element makes a modest attempt in this direction by including the examples of Chinese historians like Sima Qian and Ban Gu. A truly global history of historians' virtues, however, remains a desideratum.

gatekeepers drew the virtue card to keep women, among others, out of the emerging profession (assuming that females lacked the disposition for achieving rigour and industry). One wonders: Why was this discourse so ubiquitous? How did it develop over time and what effects did it have on historians' practice?

As these questions illustrate, a focus on historians' talk of virtue and vice encompasses more than a *Begriffsgeschichte* (conceptual history) of individual traits of character. In examining how historians talked about virtues, we discover that they were often more concerned about the order of the virtues – their relative importance and mutual dependency – than about the meanings of single virtues. Talk of virtue, moreover, frequently was a means of self-fashioning or an instrument for self-legitimization. This means that language, far from being merely descriptive, served scholars' attempts to carve out niches for themselves or to legitimize new scholarly personae such as Lerner's feminist historian and White's Camusian rebel. Last but not least, words could have consequences: attributions of virtue and charges of vice could make and break careers. This Element on historians' talk of virtue is therefore more than a study of historiographical ideals. It is a study of a historically evolving discourse that affected historians' practices in sometimes unexpected ways.

This Element is chronologically ordered: it starts in ancient Greece, Rome, and China and ends in the late–twentieth century United States. The case studies featured in this Element, however, are intended to do more than illustrate different phases in the evolution of historians' thinking about virtues and vices. They are chosen also with an eye to the more systematic questions raised: Why did historians so often speak, and disagree, about virtues? How did this discourse affect historians' practice? And how did it develop over time?

This Element starts in the ancient Mediterranean, with a section that examines when and why Greek and Roman historians invoked categories of virtue. It argues that virtues mattered among other things because of the widespread idea that texts mirror their authors' characters. This idea became so influential that scholars until well into the modern era interpreted the strengths and weaknesses of historical texts as indices of their authors' virtues and vices. Moving to China and England – two very different historiographical cultures – Section 2 shows that historians in both settings used multiple virtues and vices in assessing the merits of their predecessors, Sima Qian and the Venerable Bede. If anything, this suggests that virtues are best studied, not in isolation from each other, but as part of broader 'constellations of virtues' to which historians were committed.

The question of how categories of virtue affected historians' practice takes centre stage in Sections 3 and 4. With the example of Louis-Sebastian Le Nain de Tillemont, an early modern French *érudit*, Section 3 outlines three different ways in which the relation between discourse and practice can be studied. It pays special attention to evaluative genres, such as book reviews, which served as contact zones between historians' stated ideals and day-to-day research. In addition, Section 4 argues that the language of virtue could affect historians' practice by defining in and out-groups. While nineteenth-century German historians tried to socialize their students into an ethos of virtue, they also closed their ranks to outsiders by declaring women and Catholics, among others, incapable of developing virtuous habits.

Finally, on the basis of twentieth-century American examples, Section 5 examines what happened to historians' discourse of virtue in an age when 'virtue' began to sound like a term from the past. It argues that historians' personal qualities continued to be invoked in genres varying from methodology manuals to codes of conduct and book reviews, even though these qualities were not often called 'virtues' anymore. In the long run then, historians' continuing appeals to personal qualities are just as striking as their perennial disagreements about 'the first and most essential virtue of an historian'.

1 The Historian's Character: Why Virtues Mattered

Why did historians so often speak, and disagree, about virtues? The ancient Mediterranean world is a good place to start exploring this question, given that Greek and Roman ideas about virtues and vices have been as influential as Thucydides' *History of the Peloponnesian War* and Tacitus' *Annals*. Until well into the modern age, historians repeated the ancient commonplace that historical texts mirror their authors' minds. Drawing on Greek and Roman legacies, they believed virtues mattered because historians' characters – their virtues as well as their vices – manifest themselves in their historical writing.

In the ancient world, 'historians' was, of course, a broad category, covering a wide variety of authors who wrote about the near or distant past. For few of these authors, history writing was a lifelong occupation. Most historians turned to historical study only after retiring from military or political life. The subjects they wrote about varied considerably, as did their genres, styles, and techniques. Nonetheless, if there was anything on which most Greek and Roman historians by and large agreed, it was that history writing could, or should, serve didactic purposes. Historians recorded the achievements and shortcomings of past generations so that present-day readers might learn from them. Although this *historia magistra vitae* motif was most prominent in Roman historiography, Greek historians also granted moral exemplars a major role in their historical writing.[26]

---

[26] Mutschler, 'Sima Qian'; Duff, *Plutarch's Lives*; Hau, *Moral History*.

In this context, historians used the word 'virtue' (*aretē, virtus*) first and foremost in describing the character traits of exemplary soldiers or statesmen in times past. Xenophon, for instance, depicted the Persian king Cyrus the Great as a ruler who 'set before his subjects a perfect model of virtue in his own person' (*Cyr.* 8.1.21).[27] Livy used *virtus* almost 300 times, mostly as a word of praise for diligent soldiers, brave military officers, and courageous statesmen whom he held up as moral *exempla*.[28] This fascination for the virtues embodied by men in the past not only shows that historical writing was supposed to serve as a 'mirror of virtue', but also reflects the ancient belief that virtuous or vicious motifs were the most crucial factors in explaining human behaviour. People were believed to act in the way they did because of their character strengths and weaknesses. '*Virtus*, then, not only is something to be proud of but also works as an explanatory resource: Romans win and conquer *because* of *virtus*.'[29]

But what about historians' own virtues? Although Greek and Roman authors preferably wrote about the virtues and vices of historical actors, they realized that accomplishing this task also demanded something of themselves. Especially in writing about vices of the ancestors, or about virtues displayed by barbarian forces, historians had to be virtuous, too. They needed courage, truthfulness, and impartiality, not just to get their stories straight, but also to withstand the accusation that it was disloyal to praise the enemy or expose the shortcomings of their own people. So, when Lucian of Samosata, in the second century CE, reflected on 'the sort of mind the historian should have', courage and truthfulness were among the first qualities that he listed (*Hist. conscr.* 43, 44). Whether or not these qualities were literally called virtues, they corresponded to what Aristotle, five centuries before Lucian, had understood a virtue to be: a habitual character trait or 'settled disposition of the mind' that enables one to feel and act rightly (*Eth. Nic.* 2.6.15).

This section makes no attempt to list or classify the various virtues recommended by ancient historians. This task has recently been accomplished by Alexander Meeus, whose survey of Greek and Roman historiographical virtues shows how central notions of impartiality, truthfulness, accuracy, thoroughness, and industriousness were to classical understandings of the historian's task.[30] Even if authors of historical texts were expected to commemorate the virtues of their ancestors and uphold the honour of their country, they were also, at the same time, supposed to be earnest seekers of truth and haters of falsehood. As Cicero memorably put it, in the first century BCE: 'Who does not know history's first law

---

[27] Standard abbreviations are used to refer to ancient Greek and Roman texts. All translations are from the Loeb Classical Library series.

[28] Moore, *Artistry and Ideology*, 5–14. [29] Balmaceda, *Virtus Romana*, 8–9.

[30] Meeus, 'Truth', 90–115.

to be that an author must not dare to tell anything but the truth? And its second that
he must make bold to tell the whole truth? That there must be no suggestion of
partiality anywhere in his writings? Nor of malice?' (*De orat.* 2.62–3).

Instead of tracing the meaning and function of some of these individual
virtues and vices, this section explores the more fundamental issue of why
'the sort of mind the historian should have' was a theme that resonated strongly
among Greek and Roman historians alike. What made virtues so important to
them? And why were these virtues so often charged with polemical intent?

Perhaps the best way to examine these questions is to start with the occasions on
which Greek and Roman authors raised the issue of historians' virtues and
vices. What were the contexts that prompted them to talk about impartiality,
truthfulness, accuracy, or thoroughness? With some simplification, we might
say that historians invoked categories of virtue and vice mainly on three
occasions: (1) in outlining the contours of the ideal historian, (2) in presenting
themselves as reliable narrators, and (3) in criticizing others, past or present, for
failing to live up to standards of virtue.

Lucian's *How to Write History* provides us with an example from the first
category. Known as 'the only theoretical treatise about the writing of history
that has survived from antiquity',[31] Lucian's text is a remarkable meditation on
historiographical dos and don'ts. It did not merely insist on the importance of
truthfulness and fearless speech, but also offered a full description of the
character traits that historians had to possess:

> That, then, is the sort of man the historian should be: fearless, incorruptible,
> free, a friend of free expression and the truth, . . . giving nothing to hatred or to
> friendship, sparing no one, showing neither pity nor shame nor obsequious-
> ness, an impartial judge, well disposed to all men up to the point of not giving
> one side more than its due, in his books a stranger and a man without country,
> independent, subject to no sovereign, not reckoning what this or that man will
> think, but stating the facts. (*Hist. conscr.* 41)

These virtues appeared in the context of a broader argument in which Lucian
also highlighted the historian's responsibility to choose a worthy topic and to
write compelling prose. Interestingly, however, whereas Lucian had no trouble
stating positively the standards that subject matter and style must meet, he
defined the virtues largely in negative terms. An historian ought to be free
from prejudice, not hindered by shame or submissiveness, and unconstrained by
ties of loyalty or patronage. Apparently, for Lucian, the virtues that historians

---

[31] Free, *Geschichtsschreibung*, 2. Unless otherwise noted, all translations are my own.

needed most were *ascetic* in that they sought to suppress various forms of bias caused by love or fear.

If Lucian's text is rather unique in offering a textbook-like description of the historian's persona, more common was a second context in which historians invoked categories of virtue and vice. Following Herodotus' example – 'What Herodotus the Halicarnassian has learnt by inquiry is here set forth' (1.1) – historians liked to present themselves as reliable narrators, often by emphasizing the thoroughness of their research or the trustworthiness of their informants. Thucydides, for example, explained at some length that he did not belong to those who wrote history 'with a view rather of pleasing the ear than of telling the truth' (1.21.1). Instead, he presented himself as a man of facts, committed to sorting out truth and falsehood:

> But as to the facts of the occurrences of the war, I have thought it my duty to give them . . . only after investigating with the greatest possible accuracy each detail, in the case both of the events in which I myself participated and of those regarding which I got my information from others. And the endeavour to ascertain these facts was a laborious task, because those who were eye-witnesses of the several events did not give the same reports about the same things, but reports varying according to their championship of one side or the other, or according to their recollection. (1.22.2–3)

One of the reasons that this passage has generated much scholarly debate is that Thucydides was more of a literary artist than his so-called *Methodenkapitel* seems to allow for.[32] It is important therefore to read these lines not merely as a methodological statement but also as a rhetorical self-presentation of an author who tried to win the trust of his readers. Although such authorial self-fashioning could take on different forms, most authors tried to achieve an 'authority effect' by emphasizing their virtuous disposition.[33] Not only did they stylize themselves as truthful and impartial, but they often also stressed their care and industry or the inconveniences suffered in gathering reliable information.[34] So, in this second context, virtues primarily served as markers of serious historiographical intent.

Finally, historians invoked categories of virtue and vice in dissociating themselves from other authors, including especially their predecessors.[35] Two of the most notorious examples are Polybius' critique of Timaeus, in the twelfth book of *The Histories*, and Plutarch's critique of Herodotus, in a pamphlet entitled *On the Malice of Herodotus*. What Polybius found objectionable in Timaeus is not that he made a load of mistakes – Polybius was prepared to

---

[32] Forsdyke, 'Thucydides' Historical Method.'   [33] Wiater, 'Expertise.'
[34] Marincola, *Authority and Tradition*, 148–58.
[35] Luce, 'Ancient Views'; Wiseman, 'Lying Historians.'

forgive errors that were made inadvertently – but that Timaeus' inaccuracies stemmed from vicious habits of mind. Not only was Timaeus' sense of judgement 'childish' and 'darkened by prejudice' (12.3, 7.1); the historian often even seemed intent on distorting the truth. So, despite Timaeus making 'a great parade of accuracy', he actually departed 'very widely from his duty as a historian' (12.4d, 7.1). Likewise, Plutarch charged Herodotus with a range of vices, varying from 'personal grievance' to 'unfairness' (*Mor.* 865, 868), mainly because he found the historian guilty of withholding praise where it was due and attributing dishonourable motifs to people even when this violated the historical record. 'Thus we see how his malice, which creeps into his narrative on any excuse at all, fills his history with confusion and inconsistency' (*Mor.* 861).

Although Polybius and Plutarch were sharp-tongued critics, their practice of attributing vices to other historians was a widespread feature of Greek and Roman historiography. Josephus, in the first century CE, did not exaggerate in noting 'how the mendacity of Hellanicus in most of his statements is exposed by Ephorus, that of Ephorus by Timaeus, that of Timaeus by later writers, and that of Herodotus by everybody' (*c. Ap.* 1.16). Such polemicizing, in its turn, was not unique to historical texts. Ancient Greek philosophers and medical writers, too, were often eager to distinguish themselves from real or imaginary predecessors. To some extent, this quarrelling with the ancestors can be understood as a way of inscribing oneself in a tradition.[36] More obviously, however, such 'vice-charging' buttressed the authors' own claims to virtue.[37] In criticizing Timaeus, Polybius showed his readers how high his own standards were. 'So as the portrait of Timaeus receives more and more brush strokes, a self-portrait of the artist himself appears.'[38]

As this observation suggests, the line between critique and self-justification was thin. Emphasizing one's virtues and pointing out the vices of others were two sides of the same coin. Implied in both, moreover, was an image of the ideal historian such as evoked by Lucian. This persona, in its turn, typically served as a yardstick to measure others. The satirist that was Lucian painted his portrait of the ideal historian only after ridiculing the excessive claims to virtue made by historians who tried to fashion themselves as new 'Thucydideses, Herodotuses and Xenophons' (*Hist. conscr.* 2). The heat of polemics could thus be felt on all occasions. Even when authors offered quasi-detached reflections on the virtues of a good historian, it did not take long for the vices of others to surface in their texts.

---

[36] Marincola, *Authority and Tradition*, 219.

[37] 'Vice-charging' is a term borrowed from Kidd, 'Charging Others.'

[38] Marincola, *Authority and Tradition*, 230.

Does this imply that Greek and Roman historians spoke about virtues mainly because they sought to present themselves as more virtuous, or of higher character, than their fellow historians past or present? As true as this may be, it is only the beginning of an answer. While it explains the *purposes* of virtue talk, it does not yet explain the *relevance* of virtues to the writing of history. Why did Greek and Roman historians believe that an author's personal qualities mattered in assessing a piece of historical writing? Why did deficiencies in a historical narrative warrant the conclusion that its author had lacked virtue? The answer is that character and writing were seen as intricately related. Underlying all praise, blame, and self-presentation was the idea that historical writing reveals its author's traits of character.

Dionysius of Halicarnassus, a Greek historian born in the first century BCE, allows us a glimpse of this type of reasoning. 'The attitude of Herodotus', he wrote, 'is fair throughout, showing pleasure in the good and distress at the bad. That of Thucydides, on the other hand, is outspoken and harsh, revealing the grudge which he felt against his native city for his exile' (*Pomp.* 3). Speaking about Xenophon, Dionysius exclaimed enthusiastically: 'The moral qualities which he shows are those of piety, justice, perseverance and affability – a character, in short, which is adorned with all the virtues' (*Pomp.* 4). Similarly, Dionysius praised Theopompus of Chios not only for 'the care and industry which mark his historical writing', but also for his industriousness: 'How much effort he put into it can be judged from reflection on the wide variety of its subject-matter' (*Pomp.* 6).

In all these quotations, historical texts are understood as reflecting their authors' character traits. Dionysius could infer personal qualities from textual features because of 'the general opinion that a man's words are the images of his mind' (*Ant. Rom.* 1.1.3). What this means is that Dionysius, like many of his contemporaries, believed an author's character to be on display in his writing. Apart from that virtuous habits were *needed* for writing good history, they also *manifested* themselves in historians' prose. So, what we encounter here is a version of what Seneca, in the first century CE, believed to be a Greek proverb: 'Man's speech is just like his life' (*Ep.* 114.2). Exactly the same idea features in Cicero's *Tusculan Disputations*, where it is attributed to Socrates: 'As was the disposition of each individual soul so was the man; and as was the man in himself so was his speech' (5.47). As many scholars have argued, this assumption was a key principle underlying much of ancient biography and criticism.[39]

Plutarch was thus in good company when he read historians' texts with an eye for 'sign[s] of ill will' or 'indications by which we can determine whether

---

[39] For example, Russell, *Criticism*, 163–4; Schorn, 'Autobiographie', 682–3.

a narrative is written with malice or with honesty and good will' (*Mor.* 855).
Polybius, likewise, followed common wisdom in arguing that Timaeus' errors
'exhibit[ed]' his ignorance and pedantry (xii.4 c.1). Precisely to the extent that
historians believed words to be mirrors of the mind, they could infer virtues and
vices from what they regarded as the strengths and weaknesses of a text.[40]

The Greek and Roman examples discussed in this section show that historians
spoke about virtues and vices in assessing the merits of earlier generations of
historians as well as in presenting themselves as reliable narrators. An answer to
the question of why virtues mattered to historians must therefore be twofold.
First, virtues and vices were invoked in addressing an historian's *ethos*: the term
that Aristotle used for rhetoricians appealing to their character to persuade their
audiences of their trustworthiness (*Rhet.* 1.2.3). This strategy, however, only
worked as long as virtues were seen as manifesting themselves in speaking and
writing. Consequently, the second part of the answer is that Greek and Roman
historians spoke about virtues because they believed an historian's character to
be on display in his books.

This line of thinking proved to be tremendously influential: it persisted well
into the modern era. *Oratio speculum mentis* ('speech is the mirror of the mind')
remained a commonplace in Western culture, not only among humanists like
Erasmus ('as the man is, so is his talk') but also in later centuries. It entered the
vernacular in sayings like *le style est l'homme même* and continued to shape the
expectations that authors had to meet.[41] In his late eighteenth-century *Memoirs*,
Edward Gibbon still invoked the old *topos* ('style is the image of character') to
present himself as a virtuous scholar.[42] Even among nineteenth-century historians, it was not uncommon to invoke personal character traits in explaining the
strengths and weaknesses of historical monographs.

If this explains why both ancient historians and their successors in more
recent periods spoke frequently about virtues beneficial to historical studies, it
does not shed much light on the second part of the question raised at the
beginning of this section: Why did historians so often disagree about virtues?
Although we saw that categories of virtue were often used for polemical
purposes, arguing that someone fails to live up to standards of virtue is not
the same as disagreeing over standards of virtue *as such*. Section 2 will therefore
examine: what caused historians to formulate such standards in different ways?;
and what made them charge virtues like truthfulness and impartiality with
different meanings or different degrees of importance?

---

[40] Marincola, 'Plutarch.'   [41] Corby, 'Style is the Man', 171–3.
[42] As discussed in Roberts, 'Memoirs', 217–18.

2 What Virtues, Which Aims? Why Historians Disagreed

If historians were supposed to be virtuous, which virtues were they expected to display? How important was impartiality compared to love of country, or thoroughness in comparison to moral discernment? Was Thucydides a virtuous historian because of his commitment to 'the greatest possible accuracy' (1.22.2)? Or did his reluctance to turn historical writing into a tool of political legitimation detract from what historical study was all about? The answer depended on the goals that historiography was supposed to serve. Virtues ascribed to historians corresponded to how the 'duty' or 'office' of the historian was defined. In most cultures around the world, this office encompassed more than telling true stories about the past. History writing was also, to a greater or lesser extent, supposed to be morally edifying or politically useful. What this meant, however, and how it translated into the virtues that were seen as defining a good historian, differed across cultures. Also, it was a continuing source of controversy, especially when it came to identifying suitable models for emulation. Should Herodotus be remembered as 'the father of history' or rather, because of his lack of accuracy, as 'the father of lies'?[43]

Drawing on examples from early imperial China and pre-modern Europe, this section argues that debates over virtues conducive to historical study were, and are, often disputes about goals of historical writing. The first case study shows how virtues and vices attributed to Sima Qian, one of China's most illustrious historians, mirror different understandings of the historian's epistemic and political tasks. Secondly, the case of Bede, the eighth-century author of an influential *Ecclesiastical History of the English People*, exemplifies how historians up until the early modern period agreed on *sinceritas* (purity, integrity) being a cardinal virtue. After the Protestant Reformation, however, several historians began to argue that *sinceritas* was a necessary but not sufficient quality for good history writing. For them, *sinceritas* had to be paired with critical acumen, if only to resist the lure of Catholic miracle stories.

What these examples show is the need for historians of historiography to treat virtues and vices not as ends in themselves, but as means toward realizing goals. Historians' aims, moreover, are subject to both change and controversy: different cultures expect different things from their historians. More specifically, the case of Bede makes clear that qualities like *sinceritas*, instead of existing on their own, were part of clusters or constellations of virtues that historians were supposed to embody. This suggests that virtues should not be isolated from the larger normative frameworks to which they belonged. Only the larger picture – constellations of virtues, aims that the virtues were believed to serve – can

---

[43] Evans, 'Father of History.'

explain why historians so often found it difficult to agree on the virtues most conducive to historical writing.

What is the greatest temptation to which an historian can fall prey? According to the Chinese writer Liu Xie, the fifth-century author of a book called *The Literary Mind and the Carving of Dragons*, nothing harms historical writing more than an author who is fascinated by what is strange or uncommon. It is the charm of the eccentric that lures historians into mistaking hearsay for reliable information, sometimes to the point of presenting erroneous accounts as historiographical innovation: 'They throw out what is commonplace and pick out what is unusual, boring and digging to find support for unwarranted views, bragging that "in my book is recorded what cannot be found in earlier histories." This is the source of all error and exaggerations, the greatest of poisonous influences in writing about the past.'[44] Looking back on centuries of Chinese historical writing, Liu Xie observed that even the greatest of historians, such as Sima Qian, the celebrated compiler of a massive history known as the *Records of the Historian*,[45] had not managed to avoid this vice. Although he praised Sima Qian for 'his effort to create a factual record without evasion or omission, his comprehensiveness in covering his sources, [and] his purity of style', he added that the historian's faults had included a 'love for the strange, contrary to the spirit of the Classics' (i.e., the five books known as the 'Confucian' classics).[46] Apparently, for Liu Xie, a truly Confucian historian had to be more virtuous than Sima Qian had been in his *Records of the Grand Historian*.

In a recent article, Dawid Rogacz has argued that Liu Xie was only one of many Chinese authors who saw 'the talent of a good historian' (*liang-shi zhi cai*) manifested in traits of character that we might call virtues. Perhaps the most important of these virtues was *cheng*, which translates as sincerity, honesty, or a consistent commitment to the responsibilities of a scholar. Another often-mentioned virtue was *xin*, as in *xinshi* ('reliable historical record'), where the adjective had connotations of trustworthiness and faithfulness.[47] Even in the absence of explicit virtue talk, anecdotes like the following, from an ancient Chinese history known as *The Commentary of Zuo*, suggest that something like accuracy or truthfulness was a virtue to be cherished:

> The grand historian wrote in his records: 'Ts'ui Shu [Cui Zhu] assassinated his ruler.' Ts'ui Shu had him killed. The historian's younger brother succeeded to the post and wrote the same thing. He too was killed, as was another brother. When a fourth brother came forward to write, Ts'ui Shu finally desisted.[48]

---

[44] Liu Xie, *Literary Mind*, 92. [45] On which see Hardy, *Worlds*; Durrant, *Cloudy Mirror*.
[46] Liu Xie, *Literary Mind*, 87. [47] Rogacz, 'Virtue', 255–6.
[48] Quoted in Watson, *Tso chuan*, 147.

While these examples suggest that categories of virtue and vice were as important to Chinese historians as to their contemporaries in ancient Greece and Rome, Liu Xie's criticism of Sima Qian raises the question of what it meant to charge an historian with vicious habits. Why did Liu Xie accuse Sima Qian of straying from 'the spirit of the Classics'?

Liu Xie provided a clue when he continued his survey of Chinese historiography with unreserved praise for another Han dynasty historian, Ban Gu. Although Ban Gu's *Han History* drew substantially on Sima Qian's *Records*, the difference between the two historians was considerable. 'In contrast to Sima Qian's highly syncretic and personal interpretations, which contributed to his overt endorsement of the early Han rulers' laissez-faire government and his covert critique of Emperor Wu's authoritarianism, Ban Gu had one paramount goal: to legitimize the position of the Han dynasty in history.'[49] Liu Xie's sympathies clearly lie with the latter: 'He [Ban Gu] wrote in the tradition of the Classics and looked to the Sage as his example; his narratives are both rich and brilliant; these are his merits.'[50] The reason that Liu Xie perceived Ban Gu as a more loyal follower of Confucius than Sima Qian stemmed from his understanding of the historian's tasks. For Liu Xie, these tasks included the responsibility of identifying good and evil in the past. In his own words: 'Straightforward writing by a good historian consists in the censure of the villainous and the wicked, just as a farmer roots out weeds when he sees them.'[51] Liu Xie's Buddhist sympathies notwithstanding, such moral judgements had to rely on Confucian moral teaching. Only an historian who followed 'the principles formulated by the Sage' would be able to issue judgements that were 'clear and precise, free from both acrimony and unwarranted generosity'.[52] Apparently, Liu Xie believed that Sima Qian's fascination for the strange and uncommon had distorted his moral compass: he had obscured the difference between good and evil in the Chinese past.

Interestingly, this criticism echoed Ban Gu's own assessment of Sima Qian, in the first century BC. Although Ban Gu was prepared to admit that his predecessor had provided a 'true record' of past events, he also accused Sima Qian of disloyalty to Confucian moral teaching:

> His judgments stray rather often from those of The Sage. In discussing fundamental moral law, he ... slights the Six Classics. In his introduction to the 'Memoirs of the Wandering Knights' he disparages gentlemen scholars who live in retirement and speaks in favor of heroic scoundrels. In his narration of 'Merchandise and Prices' he honors those who were skilled at

---

[49] Ng and Wang, *Mirroring*, 70.   [50] Liu Xie, *Literary Mind*, 87.   [51] Ibid., 93.
[52] Ibid., 91.

making a profit and heaps shame on poverty and low station. It is these points which mar his work.[53]

This criticism did not come out of the blue. In 74 BC, Ban Gu had been summoned to the court of Emperor Ming, where he had been shown a copy of the first twelve chapters of Sima Qian's *Records*, known as the 'Basic Annals of the First Qin Emperor'. In response to the emperor's question, 'In the words of the evaluation passed down by Senior Historian Qian, is there anything that is incorrect?', Ban Gu had pointed out that the concluding sections of the annals, on the collapse of the Qin dynasty in the third century BCE, contained some 'words [that] are not correct'. Although these happened not to be Sima Qian's own words – the passage in question came from Jia Yi, the author of a famous essay on the Qin dynasty that Sima Qian had included in his *Records* – Emperor Ming had been sufficiently offended to issue an edict that condemned Sima Qian for having been 'far removed' from the virtue or 'worthiness' demanded of an historian in his position.[54]

What virtues then did Emperor Ming expect historians to display? Esther Klein reads the story in political terms. The virtue that Sima Qian was perceived to be missing, judging by his not altogether dismissive portrayal of Han's old enemy Xiang Yu, was loyalty to the reigning dynasty. 'What the Eastern Han emperor apparently wanted to hear', Klein argues, 'was a wholesale condemnation of the Qin (which would also be an affirmation of the dynastic legitimacy of the Han)'.[55] When the emperor concluded that Sima Qian had not been 'a gentleman with a sense of rightness' – in an older translation: 'He was no righteous scholar!' – this was another way of saying that historians could lay claim to virtue only if they helped legitimize the reigning dynasty with historical means.[56]

Ban Gu and Emperor Ming were not alone in interpreting lack of moral support for the reigning dynasty as a historiographical vice. When Yang Xiong, yet another Han scholar, judged that Sima Qian 'did not accord with the sages' and that 'his judgments were somewhat in conflict with the classics', he found this problematic mainly because these deviations 'damaged the grand Way and deceived the masses, causing them to drown in what they had heard without knowing how wrong it was'.[57] As Klein explains, this had an overtly political dimension to the extent that schismatic movements were perceived as threatening the unity of the empire.[58] Only in later centuries, under political circumstances different enough to allow the *Records* to be read afresh, could their

---

[53] Quoted in Watson, *Ssu-ma Ch'ien*, 68.   [54] Quoted in Klein, *Reading Sima Qian*, 175, 176.
[55] Ibid., 177.   [56] Watson, *Ssu-ma Ch'ien*, 150.   [57] Knechtges, *Han Shu*, 56–7.
[58] Klein, *Reading Sima Qian*, 95.

author be hailed for his 'righteous air' and 'pure virtue'.[59] As Rogacz remarks, while Ban Gu provided a model for historians in times of political instability, when emperors wanted their rule to be justified on historical grounds, historians in less turbulent periods, such as that of the Song dynasty, often found them- selves more attracted to the model of Sima Qian.[60]

If all this suggests that Sima Qian's posthumous reputation was largely determined by the issue of whether historians should judge the past in accord- ance with prevailing political views, the question remains why critics consist- ently accused Sima Qian of deviating from 'the spirit of the classics'. The short answer is that nobody in premodern China could afford not to claim continuity with the 'Confucian' classics. Although the canonization of these classics had been a complex process, they had officially been sanctioned as foundational texts in 136 BCE, when Emperor Wu had placed them at the heart of the curriculum for government officials.[61] In a context where the authority of these classics could not be questioned, it is not surprising that almost each and every historian appealed to the classics and their alleged author, Confucius, even if their understandings of the historian's tasks differed substantially. Indeed, not only did Ban Gu and his admirers invoke the classics; so did Sima Qian himself. In the opening chapter of his *Records*, he stated that his most trustworthy sources belonged to a 'Confucian family' of texts written in 'old script' (a collection of pre-Qin texts that prominently included classics like the *Spring and Autumn Annals*).[62] According to Stephen Durrant, Sima Qian even stylized himself as 'a new Confucius'.[63] Consequently, even if historians read the classics differently or defined the historian's task in different ways, they all agreed that it was a vice not to follow the model of the Great Sage.

Consequently, the virtues and vices attributed to Sima Qian do not reveal much about his actual attitudes towards Confucius or the classics associated with him. They rather show a lack of agreement among Chinese historians on the responsibilities that were entrusted to them. More precisely, these virtues and vices reflect a persistent tension between, on the one hand, historians whose primary goal was to tell reliable stories about past events and, on the other, scholars who believed that they had also a political task to fulfil.

At first sight, the story of how the early eighth-century Northumbrian monk commonly known as the Venerable Bede was remembered by later generations of historians has much in common with our Chinese case study. Although the setting was very different – Bede and his readers were firmly embedded in the

---

Christian Latin West – the question of how great an historian Bede had been was discussed predominantly in terms of virtues. Also, as in the case of Sima Qian, the virtues and vices attributed to Bede reflected the range of expectations imposed on historians: providing knowledge of the past, offering historical justification for contemporary political identities, and glorifying God in documenting the history of his church on earth. Bede's critics and defenders, however, provided more fine-grained descriptions of virtues that Bede had possessed or lacked. While agreeing that the English historian had been a paragon of *sinceritas*, they assessed his historiographical merits by investigating to what extent Bede had paired this 'integrity' with other relevant qualities, such as a healthy suspicion of 'credulity' – a vice that seventeenth-century scholars came to perceive as utterly incompatible with serious inquiry.[64]

Like Sima Qian's *Records*, Bede's *Ecclesiastical History of the English People* was a work on which many generations of historians were able to project their favourite virtues and vices. This was partly because the book had few rivals: it was a unique monument of early medieval learning. More importantly, Bede's book was appreciated because of its detailed descriptions of England's conversion to Christianity, complete with many saints' lives and miracle stories. The large number of copies made and preserved in monastic libraries in the Carolingian era suggests that this hagiographical content in particular appealed to medieval readers.[65] Also, long before nationalist historians would hail Bede as 'the father of English history', his book was read as continuing an Eusebian tradition in which the history of the church was interpreted primarily as a record of salvation, testifying to God's providence.[66] So for many readers, until well into the early modern period, Bede's *Ecclesiastical History* was 'as much a theology as a history'.[67]

In this context, Bede was not only remembered for his singular gifts of learning, but also praised almost routinely for his *puritas* or *sinceritas*. For a monk known as 'the venerable' – a honorific title referring to his piety and faithfulness – this was perhaps not altogether surprising. Interestingly, however, purity and integrity came to be associated, not only with Bede's religiosity but also with his reliability as an historian. The twelfth-century historian William of Newburgh, most notably, argued that 'complete trust' in Bede's *Ecclesiastical History* was warranted because of the author's 'wisdom' (*sapientia*) and 'integrity' (*sinceritas*).[68] In a similar vein, a high medieval chronicle called Bede not only 'most eloquent' and 'most learned', but also 'most truthful'.[69]

---

[64] Daston, 'Scientific Error', 3–4.   [65] Westgard, 'Bede.'
[66] On which see Momigliano's classic article, 'Pagan and Christian Historiography.'
[67] Ward, *Venerable Bede*, 114.   [68] Quoted in Gransden, 'Bede's Reputation', 419.
[69] Fairweather, *Liber Eliensis*, 3, 15, 67, 352.

However, as time went by, the idea of *sinceritas* guaranteeing the trust-worthiness of a work of history became more difficult to sustain. Although Bede continued to be praised for his integrity, early modern authors increasingly expected historians to display additional virtues. In the sixteenth and seventeenth centuries, the most important of these was the ability to distinguish between fact and fiction, or between reliable and unreliable accounts of the past. This ability mattered in particular because of the confessional rivalries that the Protestant Reformation had unleashed. As both Catholics and Protestants sought to prove by historical means that they were true heirs of the early church, the reliability of church historical accounts in particular became an issue of political-religious significance. As Jean-Louis Quantin and others have argued, this confessional rivalry contributed a lot to a surge of interest in historical criticism and its defining virtues: accuracy, precision, and a certain dose of scepticism.[70]

Given that Bede's *Ecclesiastical History* contained numerous miracle stories that especially Protestant authors found impossible to swallow, the vice most frequently attributed to Bede was 'credulity': the naïve habit of accepting received wisdom without applying critical checks and balances. When William Geaves claimed that Bede had been 'credulous in believing of false Miracles', he repeated a complaint made by a range of English historians, from Degory Wheare to Thomas Fuller.[71] Along similar lines, a Scottish author judged that Bede, though 'a more true and uncorrupted Writer' than anyone else, was not free from the 'Crime of believing Lying Miracles; for there are so many of them inserted in his History, that they derogate from the Credit of what is true.'[72]

Insofar as Bede was defended against these charges, this was done mostly by Catholic writers. Interestingly, however, Bede's critics and defenders did not divide neatly along confessional lines. Take the following dialogue between a Catholic ('Papist') and a Protestant, from a seventeenth-century piece of Protestant polemics written by Simon Birckbek:

> Pa[pist]: I claime Saint *Bede* for one of ours.
> Pro[testant]: You will lose your claime, for though he were tainted with superstition, and slipt into the corruptions of the Times wherin he lived, *Believing and reporting divers Fabulous Miracles, and incredible Stories,* as some of your owne men haue censured of him . . . he was an Adversarie to your *Trent Faith.*[73]

---

[70] Quantin, 'Reason and Reasonableness'; Hardy, *Criticism and Confession*.
[71] [Geaves], *History*, 22.   [72] Craig, *Scotland's Soveraignty*, 111, 136.
[73] Birckbek, *Protestants Evidence*, 202.

The authority quoted here was a Catholic theologian, Melchor Cano, who already in the sixteenth century had found Bede guilty of uncritically trusting 'popular rumors and beliefs'.[74] Also, while Birckbek, the Protestant controversialist, disapproved of Bede's credulity, he softened his critique by attributing the vice to 'the corruptions of the Times'. Fuller and other Protestants did likewise: they framed Bede's credulity as a *vitium seculi* (a vice of Bede's age) rather than as a *vitium hominis* (a vice of the man himself).[75]

If this already suggests that multiple virtues and vices were invoked in assessing Bede's historiographical achievements, another concept brought into the conversation was 'impartiality'. Seventeenth-century English historians embraced this virtue – if not in practice, then at least in theory – as a remedy to various forms of religious-political partisanship.[76] In 1620, for instance, the English Catholic historian Edmund Bolton discussed the 'Necessity of Impartiality in Historiographers.' For him, Bede had been an epitome of this virtue, mainly because of the 'admirable Justice' that the medieval historian had displayed in acknowledging the merits of figures with whom he theologically disagreed.[77] By contrast, Fuller found Bede often 'over-partial to his own countrymen', the Anglo-Saxons, with the effect of downplaying the historical achievements of the Britons.[78]

So, even if Bede's *sinceritas* was never doubted, the medieval monk was seen as only partly living up to virtues of the kind that historians in early modern Europe believed to matter most: impartial judgement and critical dissociation from miracles and myths. In the words of a later commentator, Bede had been 'an honest and holy Man, but not of the most distinguishing and accurate Judgment'.[79]

Why is it important to observe that early modern authors invoked a broad array of virtues and vices in assessing Bede's historiographical merits? Although this observation does not seem particularly remarkable, it challenges a historiographical tradition of studying virtues in relative isolation from each other. As explained in the introduction, several recent studies trace how impartiality, sympathy, and empathy acquired different meanings in different historical settings. Insightful as such studies may be, we should not forget that in actual practice, virtues always interacted. Historians never put all their cards on a single virtue and typically warned each other against a plethora of vices.[80] In addition to conceptual histories of individual virtues, we therefore need case

---

[74] Cano, *Locorum theologicorum*, 658.   [75] Fuller, *Church-History*, 255.
[76] Preston, 'English Ecclesiastical Historians.'   [77] Bolton, *Hypercritica*, 199, 213.
[78] Fuller, *Church-History*, 255.   [79] [Smith], *Britons*, 277.
[80] As illustrated also by Kivistö, *Vices of Learning*.

studies that unravel with contextual precision how scholars invoked multiple virtues – 'constellations of virtues', more precisely – in evaluating each other's work.[81]

This conclusion ties in with the observation that virtues and vices as attributed to Sima Qian reflected the goals that historians were expected to pursue. For most commentators, these goals were not limited to knowing the past. Just as the meaning and relative importance of a virtue always depended on other, overlapping or complementary virtues, so the goal of acquiring historical knowledge often interacted with other goals, such as drawing lessons from the past or providing historical justification for political authority. In many cultures, historians therefore faced the task of weighing and balancing the expectations held of them, just as they weighed and balanced the virtues seen as conducive to these ends. If they disagreed about the virtues most needed for writing good history, this disagreement often originated from differences in emphasis: from prioritizing historical understanding over moral usefulness, valuing impartiality over loyalty, or thinking that readability matters more than thoroughness.

Seen from this perspective, the two cases examined in this section illustrate a mechanism of weighing and balancing that was anything but peculiar to premodern Europe or China. When early modern humanists like Lorenzo Valla unmasked the Donation of Constantine as a forgery, it was the relation between historical knowledge and religious authority (which of the two was most important?) that determined whether Valla's sharp eye for anachronisms counted as a virtue or a vice.[82] Likewise, when David Hume complained that eighteenth-century British historians never even remotely approached the heights of Greek or Roman history writing, or when Johann Gustav Droysen, almost a century later, dismissed the popular histories of Thomas Babington Macaulay ('Neither Hume nor Thucydides has ever adopted this light tone of entertainment novels'), it was the relation between historical knowledge and aesthetic or stylistic virtuosity that was at stake.[83] Also, when a generation of European historians after World War II dissociated themselves from pre-war political history writing, they did so, among other things, because a strong commitment to democratic values made them reinterpret the virtue of objectivity as the vice of political 'quietism'.[84] So, on many occasions, historians disagreed about the virtues required for historical study, not only because virtues allowed for more than one meaning, but also, more fundamentally,

---

[81] Paul, 'Scholarly Persona', 363–5; Paul, 'Virtue Language', 708–10.
[82] Celenza, *Italian Renaissance*, 20–64.
[83] Hicks, *Neoclassical History*, 170–209; Droysen, *Briefwechsel*, vol. 2, 451.
[84] Brands, *Historisme als ideologie*.

because different understandings of the goals they should serve led historians to assign different weights to different virtues.[85]

3 Discourse Meets Practice: Virtues as Performance Criteria

So far, we have seen historians using categories of virtue and vice mainly as a language for articulating historiographical ideals. Even when they argued that Sima Qian or Bede had been insufficiently loyal or critical, these judgements reflected their views on what historians should *ideally* do more than how they themselves *actually* behaved in studying the past. This raises the question of how historians' language of virtue related to everyday realities of collecting sources, making notes, or teaching classes. What did accuracy or sharp-mindedness mean when historians saw themselves confronted with contradictory sources? How much did they care about impartiality when their country was in need or when their religion had to be defended? In other words, how did discourses of virtue as discussed in the two previous sections relate to historians' actual practice?

As the following pages will make clear, this question is not an easy one to answer. While we have no lack of sources informing us about historians' *language* of virtue, these sources do not offer transparent windows on how historians *practiced* virtues. Precisely because of their idealizing tendencies, obituaries that stylize historians into paragons of virtue cannot be taken at face value: they must be subjected to proper source criticism. Likewise, personal recollections and eyewitness accounts that depict historians as truth-loving men of learning must be handled with care. While testifying to the felt importance of representing historians as virtuous scholars, texts in these genres often deploy too many commonplaces to offer a reliable account of a scholar's actual virtues and vices. Still, even if we cannot simply infer practice (what virtuous habits scholars really displayed) from discourse (what virtues historians claimed to practice), it would be unsatisfactory to limit ourselves to discourse analysis. We would like to know: What virtues did historians practice in the library, the archive, or the study?

Drawing on the example of a seventeenth-century Catholic historian, Louis-Sébastien Le Nain de Tillemont, this section outlines three different ways in which historians of historiography might approach this question. First, they might read an historian's essays, books, or research notes with an eye to what they reveal about their author's character traits. Secondly, they can try to determine to what extent historians lived up to their self-professed ideals of virtue. Thirdly, they can examine how evaluative texts, such as book

---

[85] Paul, 'Weak Historicism', 379–87.

reviews, served as contact zones between historians' discourse and their practice. However, before exploring these different approaches, we must ask: Who was Louis-Sébastien le Nain de Tillemont, and what kind of history did he write?

A French Catholic *érudit*, born into a Jansenist family and trained at Port Royal, Tillemont belonged to a circle of scholars around Jean Mabillon, the Benedictine monk who almost singlehandedly created the field of Latin palaeography with his ground-breaking book, *De re diplomatica* (On Diplomatics, 1681).[86] To understand what kind of an historian Tillemont wanted to be, it suffices to look at the frontispiece to Mabillon's book (Figure 1) – an exercise that has the additional advantage of showing us in passing a visual representation of historians' virtues.[87]

While frontispieces of sixteenth- and seventeenth-century history books typically varied on the classical trope of *historia magistra vitae*, with historians in the role of writers who encouraged their readers to imitate ancient models of virtue,[88] the engraving facing the title page of *De re diplomatica* shows us something different. Although its motto, *veri justique scientia vindex* ('knowledge is the guardian of truth and justice'), is fairly traditional, the allegorical figures of knowledge, truth, and justice are depicted in a setting that is anything but conventional. On the left, we see a man immersed in reading, sitting in a library with a rich collection of leather-bound books on the shelves. On the right-hand side, a man emerges from the archives with an ancient scroll in his hands. Apparently, Scientia (kneeling in the forefront) cannot serve justice and truth without engaging in thorough research. The historian appears here, not as a writer, but as a researcher.[89] This is exactly how Tillemont saw himself: as a conscientious scholar whose task was not to please readers with well-polished prose, but to distil a true account out of a confusing array of partly unreliable, partly contradictory sources pertaining to the history of Rome and the Christian church in late Antiquity. Consequently, Tillemont's main works – his *Histoire des empereurs* (History of the Emperors, 6 vols., 1690–1738) and his *Mémoires pour servir à l'histoire ecclésiastique des six premiers siècles* (Memoirs Useful for the Ecclesiastical History of the First Six Centuries, 16 vols., 1693–1712) – read more like annotated source compilations, interspersed with source critical reflections, than as smooth historical narratives. Unmistakably, Tillemont was primarily concerned about getting his facts straight, without giving much attention to issues of style.

---

[86] Grafton, *Inky Fingers*, 78–104. Neveu, *Historien*, offers a book-length biography of Tillemont.

[87] On the iconography of virtues and vices, see Hourihane, *Virtue and Vice*.

[88] Kintzinger, *Chronos und Historia*, 117–23.   [89] Ibid., 181–2.

Figure 1 Frontispiece by Pierre Monier and Pierre François Giffart in Jean
Mabillon, *De re diplomatica libri VI*. Paris: Billaine, 1681. Free of copyright
available at https://upload.wikimedia.org/wikipedia/commons/b/b4/
De_re_diplomatica_17764.jpg.

Another striking feature of the frontispiece is that Scientia keeps her eyes
focussed, not on Veritas or Justitia, nor on the idealized city of Rome in the
background, but on Jesus Christ (the face with the halo). For Catholic *érudits*
like Mabillon and Tillemont, historical research and Christian devotion were no

separate spheres of life: the two were supposed to reinforce each other. As Mabillon explained in his *Traité des études monastiques* (Treatise on Monastic Studies, 1691), historical inquiry could contribute to the shaping of a Christian self insofar as it was practiced with modesty and prudence rather than undertaken out of passion or pride. These virtues, in their turn, were indispensable to a branch of scholarship that was called to serve truth and justice rather than political or confessional interests.[90] Tillemont, likewise, saw his studies as a means for spiritual growth. If he abstained from writing in a style that would make his name as an author, this was (on his own account at least) to avoid the vice of vainglory. Moreover, he believed that he would encourage his readers 'to crucify [their] vices' to the extent that he as an author would practice 'humility and all the other virtues'.[91]

The case of Tillemont thus takes us into a world where study of the past served as a spiritual exercise for author and readers alike. It was a world in which historians' virtues and vices were inseparable from religious virtues and vices. For both historians and their readers, seeking historical truth required the same relinquishing of self-centred vices as accepting the truth revealed in Jesus Christ.[92]

Confronted with such high-minded ideals of virtue, historians of historiography may want to raise a down-to-earth question: What virtues did Tillemont actually practice? Regardless of what he *said* about virtue, what were the character traits that he displayed in his research and writings on ancient Rome? There are, as said, three ways in which historians of historiography might answer this question. The first and most straightforward one is to take a volume of Tillemont's *Mémoires*, identify its strengths and weaknesses, and interpret these as markers of the author's virtues and vices. This is how many recent studies on scholarly virtues proceed: they infer virtues and vices from a scholar's published work or unpublished research notes.[93]

Along these lines, we might argue that Tillemont's discussion of Arius (to pick a random passage from his *Mémoires*) testifies to his carefulness and precision. Tillemont tells his readers that he is inferring Arius' theological views from a treatise ascribed to Athanasius, adding between square brackets that this attribution is not certain, yet most likely, and that the text is reliable because it finds support in other sources, which Tillemont cites in the right-hand margin of his text, complete with volume and page numbers.[94] Clearly, both the

---

90 Mabillon, *Traité*, 5–9, 224–42.   91 Tillemont, 'Réflexions', 114.
92 Neveu, *Historien*, 230–1.
93 For example, Van Dongen, 'Epistemic Virtues'; Kidd, 'Sir William Crookes'; Roberts and Wood, *Intellectual Virtues*.
94 Tillemont, *Mémoires*, 6:243.

argument and the annotation testify to Tillemont's carefulness. Along similar lines, we might argue that the author was not exactly an impartial historian. If Tillemont depicts Arius as an instrument of the devil, used to deceive the faithful and weaken Christ's church, we might interpret this as evidence of preconceived religious ideas.[95] Also, in a similarly critical mode, we may observe that Tillemont's habit of quoting extensively from primary sources, to the point of offering his readers a collection of source fragments more than a narrative of his own, leads to a one-sidedness of the kind that Gibbon would capture in his image of Tillemont as a 'patient and sure-footed mule of the Alps': a scholar who could 'be trusted in the most slippery paths', yet did not do much more than to offer helpful assistance to historians with greater literary talent.[96]

Tillemont's research notes, preserved in the Bibliothèque nationale de France, can be analyzed in a similar manner. They not only offer a fascinating insight into the massive reading that went into the *Histoire* and *Mémoires*, but also allow us to trace how Tillemont collected bits and pieces of historical information and used them in his writing. For instance, some of the notes that Tillemont took while reading Augustine's letters (in the seventeenth-century Maurist edition) reappear almost literally in the thirteenth volume of his *Mémoires*.[97] If this testifies to the historian's efforts to stay as close as possible to his sources, it may also serve as evidence of Tillemont practicing virtues of precision and accuracy.

Against the background of sections 1 and 2, this way of inferring virtues and vices from Tillemont's books and notes is a familiar one: it closely resembles how historians have always assessed each other's work, proceeding from the assumption that written texts (published or unpublished) reflect their authors' character traits. As a historiographical strategy, however, this procedure leaves something to be desired, not only because it presupposes a version of the ancient *oratio speculum mentis*, but also because it projects modern understandings of accuracy, precision, and impartiality back upon the past. Detecting a lack of impartiality in Tillemont's *Mémoires* amounts after all to judging the work in terms of what we nowadays understand impartiality to mean. It ignores what impartiality meant to seventeenth-century French historians, while also overlooking that, ironically, Tillemont was frequently hailed as a paragon of precisely this virtue.[98]

---

[95] Ibid., 239.   [96] Quoted in Jordan, 'LeNain de Tillemont', 483.

[97] Compare the notes quoted in Neveu, *Historien*, 226 ('Il rejette les éloges de Volusien', 'Son estime pour la profondeur de l'Ecriture') with Tillemont, *Mémoires*, 13:594 ('Ainsi après avoir répondu avec une simplicité modeste aux eloges qu'il [i.e., Volusianus] faisoit de luy, en luy representant la profondeur de l'Ecriture').

[98] For example, N. N., review (1690), 314, 316–17.

So, although it is plausible enough to say that Tillemont was careful and conscientious, the problem with this inference is that it fails to examine the relation between Tillemont's work and standards of virtue and vice as they were invoked by seventeenth-century historians themselves. To see how *their* language of virtue and vice translated into practice, we need to know what virtues *they* cared about, how *they* defined them, and to what extent *they* saw these traits at work in Tillemont's writing.

Fortunately, there are other ways of studying Tillemont's virtues. A second strategy available to historians of historiography is to examine whether or to what extent Tillemont's historical writing met the author's self-professed ideals of virtue. Tillemont's case lends itself well to this kind of analysis, as the author clearly stated what virtues he wanted historians to possess. In a posthumously published essay on 'The Qualities Necessary of a Historian of the Lives of the Saints', Tillemont argued that the historian's style should be as modest, unassuming, and self-effacing as possible. At no point should an historian 'seek to have his style and spirit esteemed'. If a sober style testifies to an attempt to practice humility, readers in turn are encouraged to do the same. Implicitly, historians thus summon their readers 'to crucify the vices' and practice 'devotion and modesty'. None of this, however, will have any effect if the historian himself does not lead 'a holy life proportioned to the holiness of his subject'. He will be able to promote humility only if he himself does what readers of saints' lives are always supposed to do: modelling themselves after the *exempla* of holy men and women. So, according to this text, it was not accuracy or precision, but humility that was the virtue that Tillemont appreciated most.[99]

Although there is a growing body of literature on how scholars practiced, or failed to practice, the virtue of humility,[100] the problem with seventeenth-century understandings of humility is that they do not allow this virtue to be attributed to individuals as straightforwardly as historians of historiography might want to. Like many others in his time, the pious Catholic that was Tillemont understood *humilité* first and foremost as a human attitude towards God. As this attitude could easily be faked for the not-so-humble sake of gaining admiration from others, devotional literature at the time often warned against 'false' humility. However, as only God knew the secrets of a human heart, the difference between real and pretend humility was often hard to tell.[101] Therefore, as long as we work with Tillemont's understanding of humility – an attitude towards God that largely escapes human perception – it is difficult to

---

[99] Tillemont, 'Réflexions', 114–15.

[100] For example, Church and Samuelson, *Intellectual Humility*; Roberts and Wood, 'Humility'; Kidd, 'Confidence'.

[101] Clement, *Reading*; Negri, *Representations*.

determine how much humility the historian himself displayed. Was it a sign of humility that Tillemont published the first volumes of his *Histoire* only under his initials? Or was this only a pretence of humility, given that every French *érudit* at the time knew what Tillemont was working on?

Someone who was not afraid of answering this question was Tillemont's biographer and former research assistant, Michel Tronchay. Quoting Tillemont on the vain desire of becoming a well-reputed author ('May God save us from this foolish ambition'), Tronchay stated explicitly that these words did not stem from 'feigned humility', but from heartfelt humbleness. To corroborate this claim, the biographer not only interpreted Tillemont's use of initials as evidence of his 'aversion to praise', but also presented a variety of other anecdotes. One of them is about Tillemont's father, who proudly told his son that the first volume of his *Histoire* had received a glowing review in the country's leading learned periodical. In a truly saint-like fashion, however, the son refused to read the piece: he did not want to put his soul in danger. So, in Tronchay's eyes, Tillemont's discourse and practice perfectly accorded with each other: 'His conduct matched his language'.[102]

Tronchay's biography, however, was a work of hagiography: it stylized Tillemont into a saint-like scholar whose life was 'proportioned to the holiness of his subject'. The anecdotes just cited should therefore not be read as glimpses of a world behind the text, but as evidence that at least some of Tillemont's contemporaries saw no contradiction between the historian's language of virtue and his actual practice. Still, in Tronchay's idealizing account of Tillemont's life, this historiographical practice is described only in general terms. The book does not offer any details about Tillemont's research habits, his source criticism, or his reluctance to impose narrative form on his material. The question therefore remains: Would it be possible to get a little closer to how seventeenth-century historians saw virtues at work in historical practice?

Arguably, nowhere did discourse and practice meet more concretely than in evaluative genres such as book reviews and letters of recommendation. Like peer review reports and thesis evaluation forms in more recent times, historians' book reviews allow us to see how scholars put categories of virtue and vice into action. To the extent that the genre measured historians' performance against standards of virtue, it served as a contact zone between discourse and practice – a space where language of virtue met the everyday reality of historians reading sources, proposing arguments, and crafting storylines. By way of third strategy, therefore, we might do what Tillemont allegedly refused to do and examine how periodicals like *Le journal des sçavans* reviewed the historian's work.

---

[102] [Tronchay], *Vie*, 50, 51, 52–3, 50.

Notably, the anonymous scholar who reviewed the first volume (1690) of Tillemont's *Histoire* in *Le journal des sçavans* had nothing but praise: he hailed the book as 'a work of research, of exactitude, of application, and of a discernment that is as astonishing as it is satisfactory'. In emphasizing Tillemont's 'exactitude to the point of scrupulousness', this first review set the tone for later ones. Without accusing Tillemont of even a single vice, reviewers of later volumes declared to be struck by 'the same care for the truth, the same discernment, the same fairness, the same wisdom'. Even volume 6, published decades after Tillemont's death, was said 'not to be inferior to previous ones in terms of exactitude and erudition'.[103] Reviewers saw this virtue of exactitude most clearly at work in Tillemont's weighing and sifting of sometimes contradictory source material. Exactitude referred to the 'utmost accuracy' with which the author differentiated original texts from later add- itions and reliable testimonies from unsubstantiated stories. Interestingly, in relation to this source criticism, reviewers also invoked Tillemont's favourite virtue of humility. Characteristic of the *Mémoires*, wrote a reviewer in 1693, is their cautiousness in establishing the dates of Jesus' birth and death, their restraint in matters of dating more generally, and their refusal to draw firm conclusions in the absence of conclusive evidence. Page after page, the reader encounters 'the same restraint' and 'the same modesty'.[104]

In two respects, these early modern book reviews resemble the critiques of ancient historians discussed in Section 1. Not unlike Lucian's and Dionysus of Halicarnassus' polemical treatises, book reviews were an evaluative genre, in which virtues served as historiographical performance criteria. Instead of denoting lofty ideals, they were invoked as standards that historians were supposed to meet. Secondly, what book reviewers assessed were not merely the books under discussion. Drawing on the trope of texts mirroring their authors' characters, they did not hesitate to interpret a book's strengths and weaknesses as indices of an author's virtues and vices. In the genre of book reviews, discourse and practice therefore clearly touched upon each other.

Like the other strategies, this third way of studying virtues in historians' practice comes with certain limitations. Arguably, its commitment to historiciz- ing virtues and vices is not only a strength but also a weakness. To the extent that it helps historians of historiography avoid projecting modern notions of honesty or impartiality back upon the past, it also denies them the right to say on their own behalf that Tillemont was a careful scholar. The only thing they can state

---

[103] N. N., review (1690), 313–14, 314; N. N., review (1691), 205; N. N., review (1738), 319.

[104] N. N., review (1695), 4; N. N., review (1693), 207.

within the context of this third approach is that Tillemont's reviewers *perceived* him as careful.

Recent studies, nonetheless, opt for the third strategy more frequently than for either the first or the second one. Scholars' evaluative practices in particular are increasingly receiving historiographical attention. Christiaan Engberts, for instance, studies book reviews as a genre in which scholars enforced or negotiated expectations regarding 'the desirable qualities, character traits, and virtues of scholars'.[105] Drawing on the book review sections of history of science journals, Richard Kremer and Ad Maas try to map continuity and discontinuity in the evaluative standards used by book reviewers over the course of the twentieth century.[106] Meanwhile, as Thomas Habel has shown, reviewers themselves were also bound to standards of virtue (as both journal editors and offended authors of reviewed books frequently felt a need to point out).[107] Like modern-day peer review feedback and thesis evaluation reports, book reviews thus show us historians applying standards of virtues to actual pieces of scholarship.[108]

4 Who Can Be Virtuous? Inclusion and Exclusion

Historians who evaluated the work of colleagues against standards of accuracy, precision, or objectivity illustrate one way in which language of virtue and vice affected historians' practice. Yet there were other, more subtle, ways in which such language could have real-life effects. This becomes apparent as soon as we zoom in on its pedagogical and anthropological underpinnings. Standards of virtue were not only performance criteria, to be applied to each and every student of history; they were also character traits that not everyone was believed to be able to develop. Ever since Antiquity, philosophers had been pondering whether virtues could be taught, to what extent they were acquired or innate, and whether men and women were equally able to develop virtuous habits of mind. The last of these issues had been the least controversial one: many believed that Aristotle had been right in differentiating between male and female virtues or, more specifically, between gendered versions of the virtues (as in *Pol.* 1,1260a: 'the temperance of a woman and that of a man are not the same, nor their courage and justice'). Even though the virtues were often allegorically personified in female form, Marie de Gournay, writing in 1595, ironically told her readers that they were blessed if they did not belong to that half of the population whose virtues seemed to consist of ignorance and servitude.[109] As long as

---

[105] Engberts, 'Scholarship', 664.   [106] Kramer and Maas, 'Tale of Reviews', 772.
[107] Habel, *Gelehrte Journale*, 231–50.
[108] As Section 5 will point out, something similar applies to scholarly controversies.
[109] [Gournay], 'Préface', iii*.

female virtues were located primarily in the domestic sphere, the virtues required for public life or the pursuit of learning only seemed accessible to males.[110]

This section draws on the case of nineteenth-century Germany, with a brief excursion to Great Britain, to illustrate the persistence of these beliefs as well as their impact on historians' practice. Historical studies in early Wilhelmine Germany were dominated by figures like Georg Waitz and Heinrich Sybel, two influential students of Leopold von Ranke. They resembled Tillemont insofar as they saw themselves primarily as researchers engaged in primary source research (or, in Sybel's case, as facilitating such research with institutional means). Also, like many of their predecessors, they used book reviews and obituaries to tell their readers what virtues they wanted historians to practice. In turn, these standards of virtue reveal how Sybel and Waitz tried to navigate the sometimes conflicting demands of scholarship and nation-state. Most important for our purposes, however, is that the two men contributed to the establishment of a professional infrastructure for historical studies, which included university chairs, salaried research positions in state-funded editing projects, and journals like the *Historische Zeitschrift* (also known as 'Sybel's journal'). By the late-nineteenth century, historical study was no longer a prerogative of wealthy men with sufficient leisure time, but a job that at least some historians – those fortunate enough to be appointed to a chair or research position – could do for a living.

The emergence of this profession gave a new impetus to an old set of questions: What are the historians' cardinal virtues? To what extent can they be taught and to whom? Although these were central questions in the sense that they touched upon almost every aspect of the newly emerging profession,[111] they were raised specifically in relation to university teaching and in controversies over the admission of non-Protestant, non-male, or non-middle class students. Although it has rightly been argued that language of virtue contributed to the development of an exclusive, 'professional' ethos among nineteenth-century historians,[112] it is important to add that this discourse had a flipside, too. Insofar as historians' virtues were understood to require a certain dispositional aptitude, women, Catholics, Jews, socialists or people from outside of Europe could easily be kept outside of the profession by arguing that only men with certain social backgrounds and political leanings could meet this characterological requirement.

---

[110] A spirited protest against this assumption, authored by Germany's first female medical doctor, can be found in Leporin, *Gründliche Untersuchung* (1742).
[111] As I argue in Paul, 'Missing Link.'   [112] Tollebeek, 'Commemorative Practices.'

Insofar as historians of historiography have studied virtues and vices in nine-teenth-century historical studies, they have drawn attention specifically to 'historical exercises' of the kind that Waitz conducted in Göttingen. Waitz was known as one of the most 'scientific' historians of his generation, in the sense that he greatly valued critical source examination over patriotic sentiment or literary skill. In an age when *Wissenschaftlichkeit* was an ambition captivating the imagination of many, Waitz's critical attitude, combined with his wide-ranging erudition and remarkable productivity, earned him the reputation of an ideal university teacher. As Max Lehmann once put it, students of his generation, born around mid-century, took it for granted 'that whoever aspires to become someone in history should study with Georg Waitz in Göttingen'.[113] This not only meant that students should attend Waitz's lecture courses on constitutional history, but also implied that they should try to get access to Waitz's historical exercises: an informal, invitation-only seminar, held on Tuesday or Friday evenings in Waitz's private study, where students read historical sources together and nervously presented their own research attempts:

> How many a young historian had the heart pounding in anxious excitement before the day it was the turn for his debut, when he was awaiting the master's judgment! But how pleasant then was the awareness of being recognized or even praised by the revered man! When the hour of exercises was over – the jocular youthful happiness of a first success, the sympathetic words and the faithful handshake of the comrades! It is not surprising that we Waitzians stand together proudly and firmly . . .[114]

As Kasper Risbjerg Eskildsen points out, it was in settings like these that aspiring historians were socialized into an ethos of virtue. When students looked back upon the hours spent in Waitz's study, as they did especially after Waitz's death in 1886, they emphasized time and again that the Göttingen professor had been an epitome of carefulness, precision, and sharp-mindedness.[115] Although Waitz was not a particularly gifted teacher, he served as an 'example', as one former student put it, by exhibiting the virtues required for serious historical inquiry.[116] Eskildsen is therefore right to argue that Waitz, rather than lecturing *about* virtues and vices, appeared to his students as a *model* of virtue, admonishing them 'to appreciate virtues, such as carefulness, exactness, and love of truth, and to detest vices, such as carelessness, vanity, and love of form, through his personal example'.[117]

---

[113] Lehmann, 'Gedächtnisrede', 78.   [114] N. N., 'Georg Waitz', 123.
[115] Paul, 'Virtues', 689–91.   [116] Weiland, *Georg Waitz*, 12, 15.
[117] Eskildsen, 'Virtues', 35.

One may add that Waitz himself was not the only example that his students learned to appreciate. Waitz also encouraged his students to model themselves after his own teacher, Ranke, whom he celebrated as a 'great master of critical research'.[118] In 1867, Waitz sent Ranke an open letter that reads like a lengthy advertisement for the philological virtues that he tried to instil in his students. Ignoring Ranke's writing style and political allegiances, Waitz presented his former teacher as an embodiment of three virtues in particular: 'criticism, precision, penetration'.[119] A couple of years later, the festivities marking the twenty-fifth anniversary of Waitz's exercises in Göttingen showed that his students had gotten the message. They bought their teacher a marble bust of Ranke, as a symbol of the genealogy in which they liked to inscribe themselves. 'Father' Waitz and his 'sons' had all descended from Ranke, 'the teacher of our teacher'.[120]

Here, then, is a first answer to the question of how nineteenth-century historians believed that virtues could be learned. Students could develop virtuous character traits by imitating their teacher, like apprentices who learned a craft by modelling themselves after their master. Although nineteenth-century historians had never heard of what philosopher Linda Zagzebski calls an 'exemplarist virtue theory', they were committed to what Zagzebski defines as the core of this theory: the belief that virtues are best acquired through emulation.[121]

This story is complicated, however, by two factors. The first one, reminiscent of Section 2, is that German historians did not exactly agree on how beneficial the traits that Waitz's students developed were. Although nobody denied that precision, accuracy, and sharp-mindedness were indispensable qualities, not everyone was convinced that these qualities were the ones that historians needed most. Even if Waitz was right in arguing that the 'spirit and art of history and historical writing' could not be taught[122] – these were talents that students either had or had not – critics feared that Waitz's focus on source-critical matters would produce historians who would hardly know how to teach a survey course or write an essay for non-academic readers. After all, this was an age in which few historians were used to writing only for fellow specialists. Even when scholars began to contribute to professional journals like the *Historische Zeitschrift*, many of them continued to write for cultural monthlies and newspapers targeted at middle-class audiences.[123] Given this social role of the academic historian as a teacher, not only of students but of the nation as

---

[118] Waitz, 'Göttinger Historiker', 260.   [119] Waitz, *Historischen Übungen*, 4.
[120] [Höhlbaum], *Jubelfeier*, 8.   [121] Zagzebski, *Exemplarist Moral Theory*, 138.
[122] Waitz, *Friedrich Christoph Dahlmann*, 5.
[123] Nissen, *Populäre Geschichtschreibung*, 317–19.

a whole, Waitz's pre-occupation with philological virtues seemed one-sided at best. This at least was what the Munich historian Karl Theodor von Heigel wanted his readers to believe when he approvingly paraphrased the ironic verdict of a colleague: 'If a Thucydides appeared in public today, a *Privatdozent* from Göttingen or Leipzig would know well how to expose, in one or another literary periodical, the lack of method of the unfortunate historian who is not a product of Waitz's seminar.'[124]

One might argue that such complaints about *Urkundionen* bred in seminars like Waitz's came primarily from older historians, such as Johann Gustav Droysen and Jacob Burckhardt,[125] as well as from relatively marginal figures like Heigel and Alfred Dove, whose nostalgia for a pre-professional era manifested itself in a penchant for the biographical genre.[126] This, indeed, is how many of Waitz's students liked to emplot the history of their field: as a gradual triumph of Rankean *Wissenschaftlichkeit* over the dilettantism of authors who valued a well-written essay in the *Allgemeine Zeitung* over a critical source edition. This storyline fails to appreciate, however, that dissatisfaction with Waitz-style professionalism came not merely from the margins of the profession. It was shared by Heinrich von Sybel, Heinrich von Treitschke, and other members of the so-called Prussian Historical School as well as by Karl Lamprecht and his compatriots at Leipzig. Even some of Waitz's own students admitted after the death of their teacher that his example had been one-sided.[127]

Does this imply that nineteenth-century historians disagreed fundamentally about the virtues they wanted to cultivate? This conclusion needs to be qualified. Near the end of the century, Rankean virtues as defined by Waitz – 'criticism, precision, penetration' – had been broadly accepted as markers of professionalism. Academic positions had become nearly inaccessible to historians who had not proven their scientific credentials with a monograph based on 'critical' primary source research. Also, exercises like Waitz's, often formalized into seminars with rooms and libraries of their own, were offered by historians across the spectrum.[128] Even Hermann Baumgarten, a political historian who had little affinity with source criticism, felt compelled to offer his Strasbourg students a seminar devoted to critical dissection of historical sources.[129] Accordingly, it would be wrong to think that German historians disagreed on *whether* accuracy or precision was important. Instead, they disagreed about the *relative importance* of these philological virtues, compared to imagination, love of country, literary skill, or rhetorical talent. In other words, while broadly agreeing on the list of qualities that an historian would ideally embody,

---

[124] Heigel, 'Zur Erinnerung', 3.   [125] Paul, 'Heroic Study', 75–6.
[126] Paul, 'Whole Man', 263–4.   [127] Paul, 'Virtues', 692–6.   [128] Eskildsen, 'Virtues', 36–8.
[129] Marcks, 'Hermann Baumgarten', 3.

historians disagreed on which of these virtues deserved to be called the most important one.[130]

This explains why historians regularly used Gibbonian phrases like 'the highest commandment', 'the first duty', or 'the first virtue of an historian'.[131] Rather than choosing between virtues, they tried to rank them hierarchically, thereby elevating some virtues over others, depending on how they conceived of the historian's task. Those who believed that more 'building blocks' (facts) were needed before historians could embark on building 'edifices' (interpretations, narrative accounts) had little reason to object to Waitz's emphasis on philological virtues. Others, however, dissociated themselves from Waitz's 'narrowly philological school',[132] not because they were indifferent to precision or accuracy as such, but because they perceived German historiography as already suffering from an overdose of them. Consequently, the relative importance of the virtues that Waitz's students cultivated in their Tuesday or Friday evening sessions depended on how historians positioned themselves in this debate.

What further complicates the story of students acquiring virtuous habits by imitating their teachers is that mimetic learning was believed to work only when students were sufficiently *disposed* towards virtue. When historians spoke about the cultivation of virtue, they often also spoke, in one and the same breath, about the *Anlage* (disposition) or *Begabung* (talent, aptitude) required for it. This is especially evident in scholarly obituaries – a genre that is notoriously unreliable when it comes to biographical accuracy, yet gives a good impression of the conventions that guided scholars' thinking about character, virtue, and virtue education.[133] Hermann Grauert, for instance, claimed that Waitz's 'characterological disposition' (*Characteranlage*) had made him fit for a scholarly career.[134] Paul Bailleu, likewise, spoke about a 'talent' that had 'unfolded itself richly and wonderfully', while another obituary writer maintained in more general terms that 'dispositions and characters' largely determine what kinds of scholars students of history eventually become.[135]

Versions of this argument were offered specifically in relation to exercises or seminars. The aim of Droysen's seminar, said one obituary, had been to 'awake slumbering powers', or to help students develop their individual dispositions.[136] Along similar lines, Alfred Stern argued that objectivity 'cannot be nurtured [*anerzogen*] if the germ of it is not yet there'.[137] Accordingly, the best thing that Ludwig Weiland, back in his student days, was said to have brought to the

---

[130] Paul, 'Ranke vs Schlosser', 37–40.   [131] Ibid., 39.   [132] Dove, *Ausgewählte Briefe*, 34.
[133] Echterhölter, *Schattengefechte*, 79–86.   [134] Grauert, 'Georg Waitz', 53.
[135] Bailleu, 'Heinrich von Sybel', 76; Schmoller, 'Zum Andenken', xiv.
[136] Duncker, 'Johann Gustav Droysen', 164.   [137] Stern, 'Gedächtnisrede', xxi.

university was his 'own inner talent': his teacher had merely 'recognized' and 'trained' these inner gifts.[138] Waitz would have agreed: he claimed that Ranke had always been attentive to the peculiarities of his students, 'moderating' and 'counterbalancing' their inclinations if needed.[139] All this suggests that historians conceived of their seminar as a *seminarium* in the original sense of a 'seedbed', in which all gardening was useless as long as the seeds themselves had no germinative power.

The idea of virtues depending on nature as much as on nurture was, of course, an ancient commonplace. Back in the second century CE, Lucian already had stated that part of what makes a virtuous historian is 'an unteachable gift of nature' (*Hist. conscr.* 34). The trope acquired new significance, however, at a time when professionalization put the issue of historians' qualities back on the agenda. It led Ernst Bernheim, among others, to warn prospective students against enrolling in history classes if their 'psychic disposition' was unsuited for the demands of the job.[140] More disturbingly perhaps, it provided the all-male and overwhelmingly Protestant community of German historians with an argument for keeping the doors of their profession closed to people unlike themselves.

Women were among the first who were perceived as lacking the dispositional ability to develop such 'male' virtues as thoroughness and objectivity.[141] As Angelika Epple and others have shown, this was not a new view of things. Insofar as women had ventured into historiography, they had often specialized in biographical writing, because this genre was seen as requiring empathy (framed as a typically female virtue) more than power of judgement (the supposedly male virtue required for histories of statecraft or warfare).[142] Near the end of the nineteenth century, however, the gradual admission of female students to German universities forced historians to reconsider this gender division. If students' discussion habits were 'too severe and pitiless to permit the presence of a stranger',[143] as a foreign observer heard in Berlin, then would not the doors also have to remain closed for women? And if seminar teaching made a demand on masculine virtues of 'criticism, precision, penetration', to what extent were these virtues to which women could aspire?

In a collection entitled *Die akademische Frau* (The Academic Woman, 1897) – a survey of positions held by German academics on 'the women's issue' – almost all contributors focussed on the issue of women's ability to

---

[138] Frensdorff, 'Zur Erinnerung', 111.   [139] Waitz, *Historischen Übungen*, 4.

[140] Bernheim, *Lehrbuch*, 507.

[141] On the gendering of these virtues, see Schnicke, *Männliche Disziplin*, 422–35.

[142] Epple, *Empfindsame Geschichtsschreibung*, 399–416; Woolf, 'Feminine Past.'

[143] Fredericq, *Enseignement supérieur*, 10.

develop the virtues deemed necessary for historical research. One of the most conservative authors, Georg Busolt, argued that women 'according to their entire nature cannot possess' such crucial qualities as 'mature experience of life and knowledge of human nature'.[144] Similarly, his Breslau colleague Jacob Caro quoted the apostle Paul ('Let your women keep silence in the churches', 1 Cor. 14:34) to support his argument that women's 'natural instinct' makes them unable to distinguish between form and substance in history.[145] Although Theodor Lindner was more welcoming, his plea for women's education also focussed on the contested issue of the *Befähigung der Frau* ('ability of the woman').[146] The female students in his classes, said Lindner, showed no 'lack of inner ability', but displayed 'passion for real learning', 'steady industrious-ness', and 'lasting diligence'.[147]

Insofar as these male perceptions of female abilities have received scholarly attention, they have been interpreted as evidence of masculine standards that prevented women from entering the historical profession.[148] In addition, how-ever, it is worth observing that categories of virtue and vice *as such* had a potential for exclusion, especially if they were grafted on essentialist notions of male and female abilities. As long as historians believed that only men were capable of developing the virtues needed for serious historical scholarship, they could plausibly argue that 'of course . . . young women could not do seminar work'.[149]

Women were not alone in facing such character-based criticism. Catholic students, too, were excluded on the ground of being insufficiently virtuous. As early as 1846, Waitz dissociated himself from Catholic historians who approached 'our beautiful Middle Ages' from a religious-political perspective that Waitz saw as 'anything other than German'.[150] Writing on behalf of 'we North Germans', Waitz summoned his fellow Protestants not to leave such mistreatments of the national past unchallenged.[151] Although in passing he also accused Constantin Höfler of 'one-sidedness and prejudice', Waitz's argument on this occasion did not yet highlight the vices of Catholic scholars: it focussed on the Middle Ages as they appeared in a book like Höfler's *Kaiser Friedrich II.* (Emperor Frederick II, 1844).[152]

Thirteen years later, however, in support of Sybel's decision to keep the pages of the *Historische Zeitschrift* closed to Catholic contributors, Waitz did invoke standards of virtue to dismiss his Catholic colleagues. At a time when historical criticism was busy correcting errors caused by centuries of

---

[144] Kirchhoff, *Akademische Frau*, 185. [145] Ibid., 186. [146] Ibid., 189.
[147] Ibid., 188, 189. [148] For example, Smith, *Gender of History*, 103–29.
[149] Charles Kendall Adams as quoted by Smith (ibid., 113).
[150] Waitz, 'Deutsche Historiker', 534, 535. [151] Ibid., 534. [152] Ibid.

'ecclesial or political preconceived opinion', Waitz believed that historians had no need for colleagues who tried to make the German past fit their party line. He showed himself irritated, moreover, by the 'enormous arrogance' with which Catholic authors downplayed the scientific progress that especially Protestant historians had achieved. Consequently, if Catholic historians aimed to enter the profession, they could do so only if they distanced themselves from all 'insinuations and derisions' and became just as objective as Waitz believed Protestant historians to be.[153]

Did the Göttingen professor lift this requirement when, in the early 1870s, he allowed Catholic students like Grauert to participate in his exercises? In a retrospective on his student years, Grauert remembered his surprise that a professor known for his antipathy to 'ultramontanism' was so friendly and accommodating to Catholics like himself.[154] In the eyes of more hard-line Catholics, however, this proved just to what extent Grauert had capitulated to the professional ethos of Waitzean historiography. Arguably, there was some truth to this view: Grauert and other Catholic historians of his generation did what they could to avoid the impression that they were less than fully committed to scientific research as advocated by Waitz.[155]

Nonetheless, in an age when anti-Catholic stereotypes were in no short supply, small triggers sufficed to revive the argument that Catholic historians were incapable of true virtue. Writing in 1883, the Berlin historian Max Lenz went so far as to argue that Catholics could never be objective as long as they were members of a church that expected them to obey the pope. Even if they wished to develop this virtue, they could become objective only by forsaking their 'highest duty' (i.e., obedience to the pope), thereby effectively becoming Protestant.[156] This illustrates a second way in which discourses of virtue and vice could exclude people from full membership of the profession. In the case of Catholics, it was not their biological makeup that prevented them from becoming virtuous, but their loyalty to the episcopate. Obedience to church authorities was perceived as incompatible with critical scholarship.

What these examples illustrate is the *discursive power* of language of virtue and vice. Nineteenth-century historians not only spoke about virtues and vices in discussing the demands that historical inquiry made on researchers' personal qualities, but also invoked these categories in patrolling the boundaries of their emerging profession. In seminar contexts in particular, they celebrated masculinely gendered virtues like thoroughness and objectivity as markers of a scientific ethos appropriate to a professional *Geschichtswissenschaft*.

---

[153] Waitz, 'Falsche Richtungen', 26, 27.   [154] Grauert, 'Georg Waitz', 95–6, 99.
[155] Mütter, *Geschichtswissenschaft*, 262.   [156] Lenz, 'Janssen's Geschichte', 237–8.

This, however, not only created an 'in-group' of male Protestant historians united by supposedly Rankean virtues, but also several 'out-groups', including women and Catholics, both of whom had to overcome many a hurdle to get admitted to the seminars in which German historians received their education.

To what extent, one may wonder, were historians from outside of Europe regarded as a similar out-group, unable to attain the virtues necessary for solid historical research? As Germany's involvement in colonial expansion was rather limited, this question is better addressed in a British context, where historical writing was deeply complicit in the country's imperial project. Inspired by Edward Said, several recent studies have pointed out that historians actively helped legitimize the British imperial project, that colonial history such as taught in Oxford served as an arena for discussing competing visions of imperial belonging, and that the meaning of many a key term in the historian's vocabulary ('people', 'progress', 'nation', 'civilization') was shaped by colonial experiences.[157] Studies on how historians' virtues were conceptualized in these contexts still need to be written. There are, however, sufficient clues to infer that from a British point of view, colonized people were even less likely to become virtuous historians than women or Catholics in Germany.

One such clue is the well-documented racism of Edward Augustus Freeman, James Anthony Froude, John Robert Seeley, and other leading voices in Victorian historiography.[158] While some of this was rather evident – Freeman made no attempt to hide his racist views – the idea that the British were superior to people from Asia, Africa, and the Middle East also manifested itself in subtler forms. Writing about Thomas Babington Macaulay's *The History of England* (5 vols., 1848), Catherine Hall argues that the book 'was engaged in the making of a liberal subject – more especially a white liberal subject'. If there was anything readers could take from the book, it was that the English people were far more civilized than the 'savage Indians of California' or the 'naked barbarians of Dahomey'.[159] What further added to this racism was that notions of character and virtue, both of which were central to Victorian moral discourse, were reserved for British men. While, ironically, employment in colonial service was seen as a good training ground for character, people living under colonial rule were habitually assumed to lack both virtue and the capacity to develop it.[160]

Against this background, it is hardly surprising that Indian students in early twentieth-century Oxford and Cambridge found themselves confronted with racial discrimination from professors, fellow students, and landladies alike.[161]

---

[157] Satia, *Time's Monster*; Behm, *Imperial History*; De Groot, *Empire and History Writing.*
[158] Symonds, *Oxford and Empire*, 47–61.   [159] Hall, *Macaulay and Son*, 288.
[160] Cain, 'Empire', 261–6.   [161] Lahiri, *Indians in Britain*, 50–65.

'Witness after witness', said a 1922 report, 'testified to the prejudice which at present exists against them'.[162] An Indian student in Oxford would later remember that 'all coloured undergraduates were conveniently lumped together in the composite category of "wogs" [westernized oriental gentlemen] or "n******", derogatory terms both, carrying with them the stigma of inferiority'.[163] Although the prevalence of such stereotypes among historians has never been examined systematically, anecdotal evidence suggests that at least some British scholars held aspiring historians from the East in very low regard. In his memoirs, historian and academic administrator Cyril Philips recounts how Indian students at the School of Oriental Studies in London were treated as 'second-class citizens'. As late as the 1940s, the director of the Institute of Historical Research denied them access to a seminar series on purely racist grounds ('I don't want any bloody n****** here').[164] What this suggests is that virtue was even more difficult to attain for students from the colonies than it had been for women and Catholics in Wilhelmine Germany.

These patterns of exclusion point to a certain vulnerability of the categories of virtue and vice. Language of virtue could easily be used, or misused, to disqualify non-male, non-Protestant, or non-European historians. This was especially the case as long as virtue was seen as requiring a characterological disposition (*Anlage*). Drawing on stereotypical images of female abilities, confessional habits, or national and ethnic character traits, historians could dismiss almost any newcomer on the ground of being insufficiently capable of developing the marks of a true historian. Jewish historians also faced such accusations, which explains why Ranke advised Harry Bresslau to convert if he aspired to an academic career in Germany.[165] Similarly, Dietrich Schäfer saw himself confronted with critics who attributed his historiographical deficiencies to his working-class background.[166] Apparently, categories of virtue and vice lent themselves well to *ad hominem* allegations against women and men with other social, political, or religious backgrounds than the Protestant North Germans whom Waitz saw as real historians, or the Oxbridge graduates who dominated the field of history in early twentieth-century Britain.

Against this background, one may wonder to what extent the declining popularity of the concept of virtue in twentieth-century academia was caused by a growing misfit between a time-honoured but elitist discourse with ample potential for *ad hominem* abuse and a growing higher education sector that, especially from the 1960s onwards, tried to be inclusive and accessible. More specifically, one may wonder how much chance of survival the discourse

---

[162] [Bulwer-Lytton], *Report*, 76,   [163] Bonarjee, *Under Two Masters*, 74.
[164] Cyril Philips, *Beyond the Ivory Tower*, as quoted in Chakrabarty, *Calling of History*, 54.
[165] Meinecke, *Straßburg*, 27.   [166] Vogel, 'Dietrich Schäfer', 10.

explored in this section had at a time when educational theorists began to redefine virtues 'from heritable, evolved tendencies' into 'cultivatable scientific habits' that students could acquire in a classroom setting.[167] If anything, these were explicit attempts to get rid of the idea that only students with favourable characterological dispositions were able to become virtuous, as well as to dismiss Waitz's assumption that most of the qualities that scholars needed could not be taught in class. Nonetheless, as we shall see in our next and final section, the virtues codified in Waitz's days persisted well into the twentieth century, to a larger degree than is often acknowledged – even if the word 'virtue' itself acquired increasingly old-fashioned connotations.

5 What Happened to Virtue? Continuity and Discontinuity

What happened to historians' virtues in the twentieth century? In light of the previous sections, this question can be interpreted in three different ways. First, it can be read as referring to the *term* 'virtue' and its vicissitudes among historians in an age that is not known for having much affinity with mirrors of virtue or warnings against vice. Did historians continue to use the term, despite Paul Valéry's declaration in 1934 that 'the word virtue is dead, or at least it is dying'?[168] Was the French historian Henri-Irénée Marrou an exception when he called his book *De la connaissance historique* (On Historical Knowledge, 1954) 'a treatise about the virtues of the historian'?[169] Did historians perhaps develop alternative labels for the demands that research and teaching made on historians' character traits? It is well possible after all to emphasize the importance of historians' personal qualities without invoking the category of virtue.

Secondly, the question can be read as one about the *kinds* of virtues that historians cherished. As Peter Novick has shown, American historians in the second half of the twentieth century no longer defined their ethos in terms of objectivity: this once prominent virtue sounded too positivist to make sense in a culture of pluralism.[170] Likewise, the time-honoured vice of vainglory ('love of fame') lost much of its power in a context where competitive funding schemes fuelled rather than stifled desires for fame. Speaking about truthfulness, impartiality, and accuracy, Dipesh Chakrabarty even asserts that these are virtues from 'another age', hardly relevant to scholars who proudly identify as Marxists or Leftists.[171] One might ask what alternative virtues historians developed in response to these developments. If Novick and Chakrabarty are right about the decline and fall of objectivity, truthfulness, and impartiality, what virtues, if any, took their place?

---

[167] Pennock and O'Rourke, 'Developing', 248 n. 4.   [168] Valéry, 'Rapport', 119.
[169] Marrou, *Connaissance*, 10.   [170] Novick, *Noble Dream*.
[171] Chakrabarty, *Calling of History*, 4, 33.

Finally, one may read the question as one about the relevance of personal qualities *as such* in an academic world that, over the course of the twentieth century, became larger, more formally regulated, and more welcoming to diversity than before. Did personal qualities still matter to generations trained in anonymous lecture halls instead of in professors' private studies? How much room was left for traits of character when historians warned their students to avoid *ad hominem* arguments? Although Steven Shapin, speaking about industrial science in late–twentieth century America, insists that personal qualities continued to matter, it is still an open question whether this is true for historians, too.[172]

Drawing on twentieth-century American examples, this section touches briefly on each of these three questions. In the absence of much relevant literature, it cannot offer anything resembling solid answers. Nonetheless, it tries to identify some relevant trends, based on a preliminary study of three genres: manuals on historical methods, codes of conduct, and book reviews in *The American Historical Review* (with a brief foray into the debate provoked by David Abraham's *The Collapse of the Weimar Republic*).

Manuals on historical methods are a good place to start. Targeted at history undergraduates and often assigned in introductory courses, they offer insight into what historians wanted their students to learn about methods, techniques, skills, or values associated with the writing of history. Also, because the genre reaches back to the nineteenth century – to Ernst Bernheim and to Charles-Victor Langlois and Charles Seignobos, whom we encountered earlier in this Element – it lends itself well to comparisons over time. An analysis of about a dozen American manuals, from John Martin Vincent's *Historical Research* (1911) and Allan Nevins' *The Gateway to History* (1938) to *How to Study History* (1967) by Norman Cantor and Richard Schneider and *The Methods and Skills of History* (1988) by Conal Furay and Michael Salevouris reveals a couple of things.

First, as conventional as the genre may be, it clearly changed over the course of the century. While the earliest manuals closely followed European models in discussing the ins and outs of historical criticism (with whole chapters on palaeography, diplomatics, chronology, and sigillography, in the case of Vincent), later ones devoted much more attention to the art of writing a good essay (with chapters on, for instance, 'plain words' and 'clear sentences'). Also, a historiographical crossword puzzle, with five empty spaces for the name of an historian who 'wrote [an] economic interpretation of the Constitution', shows that didactic formats by the 1980s had become more student-friendly than in

---

[172] Shapin, *Moral Life*, esp. 209–67.

1946, when a *Guide to Historical Method* still could stretch to 500 densely printed pages without illustrations.[173] What these changes suggest is that methodology books can well be read as mirrors of their time, reflecting how historians' educational priorities changed over time.

These differences notwithstanding, the books resembled each other in that they all discussed the historian's vocation and the demands that this vocation made on the historian's self. In this context, all of them mentioned personal qualities that historians had to possess to be capable of solid research. Carefulness, exactitude, honesty, industry, and intellectual curiosity were traits that virtually every author expected historians to have. When Louis Gottschalk in the 1969 edition of his *Historical Understanding* described 'the painstaking historian' as someone who is 'careful', has 'an eye for accuracy', and tries to provide 'as accurate, detailed, and impartial' an account of the past as possible, he said nothing controversial: earlier and later manuals alike offered broadly similar depictions of the historian's persona.[174] In tandem with this, the books warned at length against the negative counterparts of historians' virtues, such as 'the evils of haste and superficiality' and those of 'outspoken prejudice and blind devotion to preconceived ideas'.[175] Nevins sharply criticized pedantry and dogmatism of various kinds, while Gilbert Garraghan added sophistry and hypercriticism (two classic *vitia eruditorum*) to the list of vices.[176]

Although it is hard to specify *how much* the authors of these books believed personal qualities to matter, the examples offered suggest that there was broad consensus about the need for historians to bring certain character traits to their work. Later authors, moreover, were no less convinced of this than earlier ones. Writing in 1988, Furay and Salevouris still emphasized that 'there are a number of skills, habits of mind, and critical methods that make up the mental process of the good historian. These skills and attributes are essential to good history and also useful in a wide range of professional activities'.[177]

While this quotation illustrates that historians' personal qualities continued to be seen as relevant, it also shows that such traits were not always classified under the rubric of 'virtues'. Indeed, insofar as the books grouped historians' personal qualities under a generic heading, they mostly avoided the term 'virtues'. Although Garraghan offered his readers a rather traditional list of virtues (honesty, impartiality, thoroughness, critical sense, zeal for the truth), he listed them, not as 'virtues', but as 'qualities' or 'personal traits' typical of what he called a 'scientific temper'.[178] By mid-century, this phrase had gained

---

[173] Furay and Salevouris, *Methods*, 232–3.   [174] Gottschalk, *Historical Understanding*, 17, 86.
[175] Vincent, *Historical Research*, 22, 301.
[176] Nevins, *Gateway*, 22–48; Garraghan, *Guide*, 49, 190.
[177] Furay and Salevouris, *Methods*, 8.   [178] Garraghan, *Guide*, 43, 53, 55.

substantial popularity, especially but not only among educational theorists. Compared to virtues and vices, 'scientific temper' could much easier be imbued with connotations of rationality, modernity, and democracy.[179] Much the same applies to what Nevins called a 'scientific attitude', characterized by 'an analytical habit of mind', and to the 'scientific spirit' invoked by Gottschalk.[180] Increasingly, these became the labels under which American historians discussed the personal qualities formerly known as virtues. By the 1980s, Robert Daniels could speak interchangeably about 'mental skills', 'habits of mind', 'mental powers', and 'attitudes of mind', without mentioning virtues or vices even once.[181]

There were exceptions though. *The Historical Researcher* (1957) by Jacques Barzun and Henry Graff contained an entire section devoted to 'the searcher's virtues'. It argued that researchers had to practice at least six virtues: accuracy, love of order, logic, honesty, self-awareness, and imagination.[182] As this list reveals, Barzun and Graff made no attempt to stick neatly to an Aristotelean notion of virtues as character traits (imagination and logical thinking may classify as human capabilities, but not as character traits). 'In speaking of "virtues"', the authors explained, 'one is of course using the word as a piece of shorthand to suggest what impulses the researcher must curb or encourage'.[183] Although such explicit use of the category of virtue was the exception rather than the rule, I note in passing that a recent undergraduate manual, *The Princeton Guide to Historical Research* (2021) by Zachary Schrag, follows Barzun and Graf's example quite closely. In discussing historians' ethics, Schrag states that 'the first virtue of the research historian is curiosity'. He subsequently lists five 'additional virtues': accuracy, judgement, empathy, gratitude, and truth.[184] Although a pedant may, again, question whether truth qualifies as a virtue – is truthfulness not a better candidate? – the message is clear: conscientious historical research makes demands on personal qualities known as virtues.

A final point worth observing is that the *kind* of qualities textbooks expected historians to display somewhat changed over the course of the twentieth century. In light of Novick's narrative about the gradual demise of objectivity, it is not surprising that most manuals ceased to emphasize ascetic virtues such as impartiality and objectivity. As early as 1926, Allen Johnson argued that it was

---

[179] Mahanti, 'Perspective' (an article focussing on India, where the phrase made it even into the constitution).

[180] Nevins, *Gateway*, 202; Gottschalk, *Understanding*, 292.

[181] Daniels, *Studying*, 10, 11, 44, 114.

[182] Barzun and Graff, *Historical Researcher* (1957), 56–60.   [183] Ibid., 56–7.

[184] Schrag, *Princeton Guide*, 25, 27.

psychologically impossible to bracket personal feelings and beliefs when studying the past: 'A mind devoid of prepossessions is likely to be devoid of all mental furniture. And the historian who thinks that he can clean his mind as he would a slate with a wet sponge, is ignorant of the simplest facts of mental life.'[185] This did not imply that presuppositions, now referred to as 'biases', were allowed to reign free. In our sample of textbooks, only one manual concluded that historians' traditional mistrust of bias and prejudice had been misguided.[186] More typical of the genre was an adjustment of expectations. If suppression of all personal prejudices was impossible, given that 'the effort of self-awareness required to overcome bias is, for most people, superhuman',[187] historians should lower the bar but not give up the ideal. 'We cannot eradicate all bias', said a team-written textbook from Syracuse University, 'but we can do much to minimize it'.[188] Other authors distinguished between biases that could be avoided (unexamined prejudices) and those that could not (honest convictions, frames of reference).[189] While these examples suggests that virtues of restraint, aimed at curbing the historian's impulses, continued to be advocated, they also show that twentieth-century textbook authors held lower expectations of them than Bernheim, Langlois, and Seignobos had done before.

Interestingly, within the space thus created, a new type of virtue emerged. If casting off all biases turned out to be 'a psychological impossibility',[190] one could argue that historians at least should try to acknowledge their presuppositions so as to make them transparent. This is the position that Barzun and Graff adopted in 1977: 'Impartiality is a dream and honesty a duty. We cannot be impartial, but we can be intellectually honest.'[191] Likewise, Furay and Salevouris took it for granted that historians' work is influenced by biases, persuasions, and emotions. Although they warned their readers not to be carried away by them, they no longer called for suppression of personal views, but spoke about 'the ability to identify obvious intrusions of bias' and the need for historians 'to be alert to the influence of "subjectivity"'.[192] To the extent that historians were expected to acknowledge their biases rather than to get rid of them, *virtues of restraint* receded into the background in favour of what one might call *virtues of transparency*.

This change of emphasis is even more evident in the 'Statement of Professional Standards' issued by the American Historical Association (AHA) in 1974 and

---

[185] Johnson, *Historian*, 160.   [186] Cantor and Schneider, *How to Study*, 20.
[187] Barzun and Graff, *Historical Researcher* (1977), 154.   [188] Shafer, *Guide*, 169.
[189] Nevins, *Gateway*, 42; Furay and Salevouris, *Methods*, 182.   [190] Garraghan, *Guide*, 47.
[191] Barzun and Graff, *Historical Researcher* (1977), 153, quoting the Italian historian and politician Gaetano Salvemini.
[192] Furay and Salevouris, *Methods*, 4, 182, 7.

regularly updated since then. Codes of conduct resemble methodology books insofar as they codify professional standards in accessible language. Unlike them, however, the AHA Statement does not deal exclusively with historians' research. On the contrary, the piece was written in response to a chorus of complaints about violations of rights in hiring procedures, tenure decisions, and hierarchical forms of academic governance. Accordingly, the statement spent many more words on anti-discrimination and participatory policies than on historical methods. As these were areas in which the language of virtue was not nearly as established as in the genre of methodology manuals, one might expect that the AHA code in its various incarnations (1974, 1987, 1990) spoke less explicitly about historians' virtues than the books examined so far.[193]

This, however, turns out not to be the case. Even if the word 'virtue' was absent, the code did invoke a range of personal qualities, especially in specifying what it meant to show collegial respect. Job interviews, for instance, should be done with 'frankness and respect for individual dignity on both sides', just as candidates for promotion or tenure should be evaluated 'conscientiously' by 'disinterested' scholars. Likewise, 'fairness' should be prioritized in academic decision-making.[194] In a similar vein, the 1974 text stipulated that professors must judge their students' work with 'fairness' and 'open-mindedness'. Speaking about integrity in the classroom, the code highlighted the importance of presenting diverging interpretations 'with intellectual honesty'.[195] The 1990 version added to this that historians are obliged to present their professional credentials *'accurately and honestly* in all contexts'.[196] Even if the virtues invoked here only partly overlapped with those featured in the methodology manuals, the code shared the books' assumption that historians need certain personal qualities to do their work with integrity.

More specifically, the code testifies to the growing appreciation of what I call virtues of transparency. For instance, in addressing the vexed issue of historians' bias, the text of 1974 did not summon AHA members to overcome their prejudices, but to develop 'an awareness of one's own bias'.[197] This awareness, moreover, was not presented as a means for enhancing integrity, but as a step towards fostering intellectual plurality in the historical profession. As section 8 declared: 'The political, social, religious, and ideological beliefs of historians, when applied with professional integrity, may furnish organizing principles for scholarship and teaching.'[198] Along similar lines, the version of 1987 urged

---

[193] While the 1987 revision amounted to a total rewriting of the text, the 1990 revision only added three new paragraphs.

[194] AHA, 'Statement' (1974), §§ 15, 16, 2.   [195] Ibid., § 6.

[196] AHA, 'Statement' (1990), § 5 (emphasis in original).   [197] AHA, 'Statement' (1974), § 6.

[198] Ibid, § 8.

historians to 'welcome rather than deplore' intellectual diversity, as it 'enhances the historical imagination and contributes to the development and vitality of the study of the past'.[199] This was a position close to Cantor's and Schneider's: 'Far from bewailing the historian's "bias" and "prejudice," we have come to realize that it is the entry of the historian's mind into the remains of the past.'[200] In other words, instead of bemoaning that historians are people with beliefs and emotions, the code tried to foster an academic environment in which many flowers could bloom, intellectually as well as socially. (The 1974 version even devoted a section to historians' freedom to choose their own 'life styles' and 'modes of dress'.)[201]

The AHA code thereby illustrates what the German philosopher Otto Friedrich Bollnow already observed in 1958, namely that new virtues (such as fairness and camaraderie) were in the process of replacing older ones (such as modesty and loyalty). Even if these new qualities were no longer labelled as virtues, they resembled their nineteenth-century predecessors in being traits of character that were seen as demanded by the times.[202] Along these lines, one might argue that the prominence of fairness and honesty in the AHA code reflected the challenges that American historians were facing in the 1970s, including in particular the challenge of coming to terms with an increasingly fractured historiographical landscape, just as the value attached to objectivity in the years around 1900 had mirrored the concerns of historians who had tried to 'professionalize' the field.[203] Although the AHA statement of 1974 claimed that its standards reflected 'opinions and values developed by historians over a long period of time',[204] the virtues it commended were actually quite typical for the 1970s.

Given that both methodology books and codes of conduct specified standards that scholars were supposed to meet, it is perhaps not surprising that these genres paid ample attention to historians' personal qualities. One may wonder, however, to what extent this also applies to book reviews as published in *The American Historical Review* (*AHR*). Did late–twentieth century book reviewers still have the habit of evaluating books in terms of virtues? Existing scholarship provides us with an ambiguous picture. On the one hand, Mark Day argues that *AHR* reviewers as late as 2006 invoked dozens of 'historiographical virtues'.[205] Sjang ten Hagen, on the other hand, notices that such virtues did not always refer to historians' character traits. Already by the early twentieth century, *AHR*

---

[199] AHA, 'Statement' (1987), 106.   [200] Cantor and Schneider, *How to Study*, 20.
[201] AHA, 'Statement' (1974), § 13.   [202] Bollnow, *Wesen*, 13–6.
[203] Novick, *Noble Dream*, 469–521, 47–60.   [204] AHA, 'Statement' (1974), preamble.
[205] Day, *Philosophy of History*, 22–4.

reviewers ascribed traits like objectivity and carefulness not only to authors but also to arguments or books (as in 'an objective account').[206] Against this background, it makes sense to inquire whether *AHR* book reviewers in the late twentieth century still used categories of virtue and, if so, to what extent they were talking about personal qualities.

The *AHR* book review section of October 1983 allows for three observations. First, most of the 221 reviews published in this section kept silent about historians' personal qualities. They focussed on sources, methods, explanatory strengths and weaknesses, or attractiveness of style, without making any inference about the authors' characters. Nonetheless, several dozens of reviews expressed their approval or criticism in terms of virtues and vices. Scholars were praised for their 'incisive objectivity' (1100) or chastised for being 'inaccurate' (1073).[207] One review applauded Bettina Aptheker's 'honesty about her own assumptions and commitments' (1056), while another complimented Peter Christoff for his 'unique balance between objectivity and a sympathetic understanding' (1027). These were personal qualities similar to those commended in methodology books and in the AHA statement.

Secondly, the sample confirms Ten Hagen's observation about reviewers ascribing virtues to arguments or storylines. Although 'fairmindedness' (986) was clearly a personal quality, 'solid research, objective discussion, and analytical sophistication' (1003) were features of books, not of authors. While 'accurate' could be a trait of character, the adjective was also applied to titles (1016), books (1034), narratives (986, 1060), and interpretations (1045). This move away from Aristotelian character traits is even clearer in the case of 'careful', an epithet that reviewers used preferably in phrases like 'careful reading' (1118), 'careful research' (1018, 1024), and 'careful analysis' (970, 1014, 1035, 1039, 1119). Instead of denoting an authorial character trait, the adjective expressed how well historians had done their research – whether they had 'carefully connected [their] findings to the existing literature' (1116) or undertaken a 'painstakingly careful reading' of their source material (1118). Judging by these examples, it seems as if reviewers continued to use language of virtue, yet tried to avoid *ad hominem* inferences about historians' character traits.

Nonetheless, even if this was true for many reviewers, some of the most sharp-tongued among them did not fit this picture: they brought the personal back into the conversation by accusing authors of biases or prejudices. Leonard Gordon, for instance, did not merely notice 'a neglect of the political context' in Paul Greenough's account of the Bengal famine of the 1940s, but proceeded to

---

[206] Ten Hagen, 'Evaluating Knowledge.'

[207] Page numbers in brackets refer to *The American Historical Review* 88, no. 4 (1983). Space does not permit me to provide bibliographical details for each individual review.

attribute this neglect to the author's personal 'bias' (1051). Likewise, in a review of James Whorton's history of American health reform, Richard Schwartz assessed how much 'sympathetic objectivity' the author had been able to muster: 'Whorton makes a valiant effort that in my grade book merits a solid B plus.' He would have deserved an A only if he had managed to restrain 'his personal prejudices' (1066). Both reviewers thus invoked personal qualities, or the lack thereof, to explain perceived deficiencies of the works.

Examples of such inferential reasoning can also be found in the journal's 'Communications' section, which allowed historians to respond to book reviews that they found wanting. The last three letters in the section of October 1983 merit special attention, as they helped launch a controversy known as the 'David Abraham case.' What matters for our purposes is not the scope of this debate, which quickly broadened from factual inaccuracies in David Abraham's *The Collapse of the Weimar Republic* (1981) to the ethical standards of the American historical profession as a whole.[208] What is worth observing, however, is that Henry Turner's letter in the *AHR* attributed factual errors to flaws of character even more straightforwardly than the reviews just cited. For Turner, Abraham's 'faulty and misleading' scholarship was evidence of the author's 'slovenliness' and 'tendentious misconstrual' of the historical record (1143) – a charge that Abrahams interpreted as a personal assault on his 'commitment to meeting the demands of serious historical scholarship' (1145).

Another critic, Gerald Feldman, went even further in accusing Abraham of 'sloppiness, incompetence, tendenditiousness [sic], and untruthfulness'.[209] Writing in the journal *Central European History*, he attributed Abraham's interpretive errors to his 'indifference to what documents actually say and his fanatical attachment to his preconceived notions'.[210] In a similar vein, Feldman accused Abraham of 'considerable indifference to precision and accuracy'.[211] As commentators did not fail to notice, this extended the debate to the realm of character flaws.[212] The fact that Turner's and Feldman's interventions themselves were widely perceived as unprofessional only added to this.[213] It transformed a specialized debate about sources from the Weimar Republic into a more general controversy about the qualities demanded of historians.

So, what happened to historians' virtues in the twentieth century? This section has identified two changes. First, the term 'virtue' largely fell into disuse.

---

[208] See Novick, *Noble Dream*, 612–21.
[209] Circular letter (28 November 1983) quoted in Abraham, 'Reply', 179.
[210] Feldman, 'Collapse', 170.   [211] Feldman, 'Response', 250.
[212] Nolan, 'Clarifying', 90; De Grazia, 'Gerald Feldman Case', 81.
[213] Eley, 'Misrepresenting'; Mayer, 'Letter.'

'Scientific temper' and 'mental skills' emerged as new labels for traits of character formerly known as virtues. Secondly, in methodology manuals and codes of conduct alike, nineteenth-century virtues like objectivity gradually receded into the background. Virtues of restraint, aimed at suppressing historians' biases, made way for virtues of transparency: honest acknowledgment of the biases inherent to historians' subject positions. In addition, this section has shown that virtues played different roles in different genres. The relatively rare instances in which book reviewers attributed the defects of a monograph to the character flaws of its author show that personal qualities were invoked on particular occasions – not always, but only if there were specific reasons for doing so. Twentieth-century historians appealed to personal qualities mostly in specifying the marks of a good historian and in explaining perceived breaches of professionalism.

Most significant, however, is the finding that historians' virtues, contrary to popular perception, did not end up in irrelevance. Even if the *word* 'virtue' acquired increasingly old-fashioned connotations, historians continued to talk about character traits *as such*. This is evident not merely from the persistence of virtue terms like 'accuracy' (which sometimes lost its original meaning in being applied to arguments or narratives instead of human characters), but also and especially from historians' continuous appeal to traits of character that they saw as indispensable for responsible historical study. From the 1970s onwards, even the new genre of codes of conduct emphasized the importance of frankness, open-mindedness, fairness, and honesty. Virtues, in other words, persisted throughout the twentieth century, even if sometimes in different guises than before.

Conclusion

Historians' virtues are a theme of all times. Students assigned to read the newest edition of John Tosh's *The Pursuit of History* (2022) are by no means the first who are encouraged to examine themselves if they possess 'the qualities of a historian'. As the preceding pages have made clear, Tosh's handbook is but the newest addition to a pile of manuals that tell historians to cultivate certain personal qualities – impartiality, honesty, fairmindedness – to do their work professionally. These manuals in turn echo a view that was shared already by Greek and Roman historians, namely that good history writing not only requires a worthy topic and a decent style, but also an historian who is committed to working hard, reading carefully, judging scrupulously, and keeping biases in check. If we wonder why historians, past and present, so often speak about virtues needed for historical study, a first answer is therefore that they invoke them to instil in their students an ethos of responsible history writing.

This, however, is not the only answer. In Section 1, we saw Greek and Roman historians distancing themselves from the alleged vices of their predecessors to bolster their own claims to reliability. Language of virtue could thus also serve self-advertising purposes, just as it could serve the political purposes of male, Protestant historians who preferred to keep the doors of their emerging profession closed to scholars unlike themselves (Section 4). Equally if not more important is the observation that historians wrote about virtues and their negative counterparts, the vices, because they found themselves disagreeing on the meaning of *sinceritas*, the feasibility of objectivity, or the relative importance of precision. Sections 2 and 4 featured examples of scholars who argued about such qualities because they held different views on the historian's vocation. Catalogues of virtues are therefore often also indicative of how historians define their responsibilities or, more specifically, how they understand the relation between such different aims as acquiring knowledge, offering moral guidance, and providing political instruction. Historians, in other words, appeal to virtues not only in teaching their students how to be good historians but also, more basically, to explain how they conceive of their task and what demands this understanding of the job makes on historians' character traits.

If virtues in these examples come close to historiographical ideals, historians' personal qualities (whether or not explicitly labelled as 'virtues') also impact the mundane realities of historians' everyday work: reading, taking notes, drafting a book chapter, and preparing for a class. If virtues are character traits, they will manifest themselves in everything historians do. As argued in Section 3, such practicing of virtues, though typically not open to direct observation, can be studied in different ways. Book reviews, for instance, often use accuracy, impartiality, and honesty as performance criteria in evaluating historians' work, thereby serving as a contact zone between discourse and practice. One should be aware, though, that modern book reviewers sometimes invoke such old virtues in rather untraditional ways, as denoting qualities of texts rather than qualities of authors. Although categories of virtue persisted throughout the twentieth century, Section 5 showed that American historians in the 1980s displayed a greater reluctance to employ this idiom for *ad hominem* purposes than many of their predecessors.

This is not the only discontinuity that the preceding pages have brought into view. Apart from that, changing epistemological beliefs and transformations in the organization of historical studies affected the catalogues of virtues that historians most appreciated, the relation between historical inquiry and virtuous conduct fundamentally changed over time. As long as the past was understood as a reservoir of moral *exempla*, historical study could serve as a school of virtue. This explains why Tillemont and his colleagues in early modern France not only expected historians to bring certain virtues to their work, but also hoped to grow in virtue by studying the past. This aspiration almost totally disappeared when the *historia magistra vitae* model lost its prominence and historical study became a profession. Virtuous conduct ceased to be a goal of historical studies, though it continued to serve as means for realizing other goals. In an age that saw universities expand and open their doors to traditionally underrepresented groups of students, another time-honoured view was also abandoned: women were no longer denied the dispositional aptitude needed for developing virtuous habits of mind.

But important as these discontinuities may be, equally striking are the long-term continuities that this Element has identified. Whether or not they were literally called 'virtues', historians' personal qualities mattered throughout history, from Herodotus to Hayden White and from Sima Qian to book reviewers in *The American Historical Review*. Given that different understandings of the historian's task translated into different rankings of virtues, historians often quarrelled about 'the first and most essential virtue of an historian'. If such polemics show that the language of virtue often served as an idiom for talking about the aims of historical study, they also illustrate that historians from Thucydides and Ban Gu to Gerda Lerner and David Abraham agreed, in one way or another, that historical study makes demands on the character of its practitioners. A good historian not only possesses palaeographic skills and proficiency in foreign languages, but also is honest, fair-minded, unbiased, or intellectually courageous. Historical study requires more than methods, skills, and abilities: it also demands character traits historically known as virtues.

Bibliography

Abraham, David, 'A Reply to Gerald Feldman', *Central European History* 17, no. 2–3 (1984), 178–244.

American Historical Association, 'Statement of Professional Standards' (1974), online at ethicscodescollection.org/detail/182f3360-7ced-4bfe-a4e1-cceb6e004695.

'AHA Statement on Standards of Professional Conduct', *The History Teacher* 21, no. 1 (1987), 105–9.

'Statement on Standards of Professional Conduct' (1990), online at ethics codescollection.org/detail/85380f5c-15ae-4608-afce-c6f95bfb78ae.

Armitage, David, 'What's the Big Idea? Intellectual History and the *longue durée*', *History of European Ideas* 38, no. 4 (2012), 493–507.

Baehr, Jason, *The Inquiring Mind: On Intellectual Virtues and Virtue Epistemology*. Oxford: Oxford University Press, 2011.

Bailleu, Paul, 'Heinrich von Sybel, geb. 2. December 1817 zu Düsseldorf, gest. 1. August 1895 zu Marburg', *Deutsche Rundschau* 85 (1895), 58–76.

Balmaceda, Catalina, *Virtus Romana: Politics and Morality in the Roman Historians*. Chapel Hill, NC: University of North Carolina Press, 2017.

Barzun, Jacques and Henry A. Graff, *The Modern Researcher*. New York: Harcourt, Brace, Javanovich, 1957.

The Modern Researcher, 4th ed. New York: Harcourt, Brace, Javanovich, 1977.

Behm, Amanda, *Imperial History and the Global Politics of Exclusion: Britain, 1880–1940*. London: Palgrave Macmillan, 2018.

Bernheim, Ernst, *Lehrbuch der historischen Methode: Mit Nachweis der wichtigsten Quellen und Hülfsmittel zum Studium der Geschichte*. Leipzig: Duncker & Humblot, 1889.

Birckbek, Simon, *The Protestants Evidence, Taken Out of Good Records . . .* London: Robert Milbourne, 1635.

Bod, Rens, Jeroen van Dongen, Sjang L. ten Hagen, Bart Karstens, and Emma Mojet, 'The Flow of Cognitive Goods: A Historiographical Framework for the Study of Epistemic Transfer', *Isis* 110, no. 3 (2019), 483–96.

Bollnow, Otto Friedrich, *Wesen und Wandel der Tugenden*. Frankfurt am Main: Ullstein, 1958.

Bolton, Edmund, *Hypercritica; or a Rule of Judgment for Writing, or Reading our History's . . .* Oxford: Ant. Hall, 1722.

Bonarjee, N. B., *Under Two Masters*. London: Oxford University Press, 1970.

Brands, M. C., *Historisme als ideologie: het 'onpolitieke' en 'anti-normatieve' element in de Duitse geschiedwetenschap*. Assen: Van Gorcum, 1965.

[Bulwer-Lytton, Neville et al.], *Report of the Committee on Indian Students 1921–22*. London: India Office, 1922.

Cain, Peter J., 'Empire and the Languages of Character and Virtue in Later Victorian and Edwardian Britain', *Modern Intellectual History* 4, no. 2 (2007), 249–73.

Cano, Melchior, *Locorum theologicorum libri duodecim*. Venice: Haeredes Melchioris Sessae, 1562.

Cantor, Norman F. and Richard I. Schneider, *How to Study History*. Arlington Heights, IL: AHM Publishing, 1967.

Celenza, Christopher S., *The Italian Renaissance and the Origins of the Modern Humanities: An Intellectual History, 1400–1800*. Cambridge: Cambridge University Press, 2021.

Chakrabarty, Dipesh, *The Calling of History: Sir Jadunath Sarkar and His Empire of Truth*. Chicago, IL: University of Chicago Press, 2015.

Church, Ian M. and Peter L. Samuelson, *Intellectual Humility: An Introduction to the Philosophy and Science*. London: Bloomsbury, 2017.

Clement, Jennifer, *Reading Humility in Early Modern England*. London: Routledge, 2015.

Corby, James, 'Style is the Man: Meillassoux, Heidegger, and Finitude', in Ivan Callus, James Corby, and Gloria Lauri-Lucente (eds.), *Style in Theory: Between Literature and Philosophy*. London: Bloomsbury, 2013, 163–86.

Craig, Thomas, *Scotland's Soveraignty Asserted ...* trans. Geo. Ridpath. London: Andrew Bell, 1695.

Creyghton, Camille, Pieter Huistra, Sarah Keymeulen, and Herman Paul, 'Virtue Language in Historical Scholarship: The Cases of Georg Waitz, Gabriel Monod and Henri Pirenne', *History of European Ideas* 42, no. 7 (2016), 924–36.

Daniels, Robert V., *Studying History: How and Why*, 3rd ed. Englewood Cliffs, NJ: Prentice-Hall, 1981.

Daston, Lorraine, 'Scientific Error and the Ethos of Belief', *Social Research* 72, no. 1 (2005), 1–28.

Daston, Lorraine and Peter Galison, *Objectivity*. New York: Zone Books, 2007.

Day, Mark, *The Philosophy of History: An Introduction*. London: Continuum, 2008.

De Grazia, Victoria, 'The Gerald Feldman Case', *Radical History Review* 32 (1985), 79–81.

De Groot, Joanna, *Empire and History Writing in Britain c. 1750–2012*. Manchester: Manchester University Press, 2013.

Domanska, Ewa, 'Historians Must Have Virtues: A Conversion with the Polish Historian and Theorist of History', *Rethinking History* 15, no. 3 (2011), 419–30.

Dove, Alfred, *Ausgewählte Briefe*, ed. Oswald Dammann. Munich: F. Bruckmann, 1925.

Droysen, Johann Gustav, *Briefwechsel*, ed. Rudolf Hübner, 2 vols. Osnabrück: Biblio-Verlag, 1935.

Duff, Tim, *Plutarch's Lives: Exploring Virtue and Vice*. Oxford: Clarendon Press, 1999.

Duncker, Max, 'Johann Gustav Droysen', *Preußische Jahrbücher* 54 (1884), 134–67.

Durrant, Stephen W., *The Cloudy Mirror: Tension and Conflict in the Writings of Sima Qian*. Albany, NY: State University of New York Press, 1995.

'Truth Claims in *Shiji*', in Helwig Schmidt-Glintzer, Achim Mittag, and Jörn Rüsen (eds.), *Historical Truth, Historical Criticism, and Ideology: Chinese Historiography and Historical Culture from a New Comparative Perspective*. Leiden: Brill, 2004, 93–113.

Echterhölter, Anna, *Schattengefechte: Genealogische Praktiken in Nachrufen auf Naturwissenschaftler (1710–1860)*. Göttingen: Wallstein, 2012.

Eley, Geoff, 'Misrepresenting Abraham's Argument', *Radical History Review* 32 (1985), 77–9.

Engberts, Christiaan, *Scholarly Virtues in Nineteenth-Century Sciences and Humanities: Loyalty and Independence Entangled*. Cham: Palgrave Macmillan, 2022.

'Scholarship, Community Formation and Book Reviews: The *Literarisches Centralblatt* as Arena and Meeting Place', *Studia Historiae Scientiarum* 20 (2021), 651–79.

Epple, Angelika, *Empfindsame Geschichtsschreibung: Eine Geschlechergeschichte der Historiographie zwischen Aufklärung und Historismus*. Cologne: Böhlau, 2003.

Eskildsen, Kasper Risbjerg, 'Commentary: Scholarship as a Way of Life: Character and Virtue in the Age of Big Humanities', *History of Humanities* 1, no. 2 (2016), 387–97.

'Inventing the Archive: Testimony and Virtue in Modern Historiography', *History of Human Sciences* 26, no. 4 (2013), 8–26.

'Virtues of History: Exercises, Seminars, and the Emergence of the German Historical Discipline, 1830–1900', *History of Universities* 34, no. 1 (2021), 27–40.

Evans, J. A. S., 'Father of History or Father of Lies: The Reputation of Herodotus', *The Classical Journal* 64, no. 1 (1968), 11–17.

Fairweather, Janet (trans.), *Liber Eliensis: A History of the Isle of Ely from the Seventh Century to the Twelfth: Compiled by a Monk of Ely in the Twelfth Century.* Woodbridge: Boydell Press, 2005.

Feldman, Gerald D., 'A Collapse in Weimar Scholarship', *Central European History* 17, no. 2–3 (1984), 159–77.

'A Response to David Abraham's "Reply"', *Central European History* 17, no. 2–3 (1984), 245–67.

Forsdyke, Sara, 'Thucydides' Historical Method', in Sara Forsdyke, Edith Foster, and Ryan Balot (eds.), *The Oxford Handbook of Thucydides*. Oxford: Oxford University Press, 2007, 19–38.

Fredericq, Paul, *L'enseignement supérieur de l'histoire: notes et impressions de voyage*. Ghent: J. Vuylsteke; Paris: Félix Alcan, 1899.

Free, Alexander, *Geschichtsschreibung als Paideia: Lukians Schrift 'Wie man Geschichte schreiben soll' in der Bildungskultur des 2. Jhs. n. Chr.* Munich: C. H. Beck, 2015.

Frensdorff, Ferdinand, 'Zur Erinnerung an Ludwig Weiland', *Hansische Geschichtsblätter* 22 (1894), 107–26.

Fuller, Thomas, *Church-History of Britain from the Birth of Jesus Christ until the Year M.DC.XLVIII*. London: Iohn Williams, 1655.

Furay, Conal, and Michael J. Salevouris, *The Methods and Skills of History: A Practical Guide*. Arlington Heights, IL: H. Davidson, 1988.

Garraghan, Gilbert J., *A Guide to Historical Method*, ed. Jean Delanglez. New York: Fordham University Press, 1946.

Garritzen, Elise, 'Pasha and His Historic Harem: Edward A. Freeman, Edith Thompson and the Gendered Personae of Late-Victorian Historians', in Paul, *How to Be a Historian*, 89–106.

[Geaves, William], *The History of the Church of Great Britain, from the Birth of Our Saviour untill the Year of our Lord, 1667*. London: Philip Chetwin, 1674.

Gottschalk, Louis, *Understanding History: A Primer of Historical Method*, 2nd ed. New York: Alfred A. Knopf, 1969.

[Gournay, Marie de], 'Préface sur les essais de Michel seigneur de Montaigne, par sa fille d'alliance', in Montaigne, *Les essais*, rev. ed. Paris: Abel l'Angelier, 1595, i*–xviii*.

Grafton, Anthony, *Inky Fingers: The Making of Books in Early Modern Europe*. Cambridge, MA: Harvard University Press, 2020.

Gransden, Antonia, 'Bede's Reputation as an Historian in Medieval England', *The Journal of Ecclesiastical History* 32, no. 4 (1981), 397–425.

Grauert, Herm[ann], 'Georg Waitz', *Historisches Jahrbuch* 8 (1887), 48–100.

Habel, Thomas, *Gelehrte Journale und Zeitungen der Aufklärung: Zur Entstehung, Entwicklung and Erschließung deutschsprachiger Rezensionszeitschriften des 18. Jahrhunderts*. Bremen: Lumière, 2007.

Hall, Catherine, *Macaulay and Son: Architects of Imperial Britain*. New Haven, CT: Yale University Press, 2012.

Hardy, Grant, *Worlds of Bronze and Bamboo: Sima Qian's Conquest of History*. New York: Columbia University Press, 1999.

Hardy, Nicholas, *Criticism and Confession: The Bible in the Seventeenth-Century Republic of Letters*. Oxford: Oxford University Press, 2017.

Hau, Lisa Irene, *Moral History from Herodotus to Diodorus Siculus*. Edinburgh: Edinburgh University Press, 2016.

Heigel, Karl Theodor, 'Zur Erinnerung an Heinrich v. Treitschke', *Beilage zur Allgemeinen Zeitung* (25 June 1898), 1–5.

Hicks, Philip Stephen, *Neoclassical History and English Culture: From Clarendon to Hume*. Basingstoke: Macmillan, 1996.

[Höhlbaum, Konstantin], *Die Jubelfeier der historischen Übungen zu Göttingen am 1. August 1874: Bericht des Fest-Comités*. Göttingen: Fr. W. Kästner, 1874.

Hourihane, Colum (ed.), *Virtue and Vice: The Personifications in the Index of Christian Art*. Princeton, NJ: Princeton University Press, 2000.

Hursthouse, Rosalind and Glen Pettigrove, 'Virtue Ethics', *The Stanford Encyclopedia of Philosophy* (2018), online at https://plato.stanford.edu/archives/win2018/entries/ethics-virtue.

Johnson, Allen, *The Historian and Historical Evidence*. New York: Charles Scribner's Sons, 1926.

Jordan, David P., 'LeNain de Tillemont: Gibbon's "Sure-Footed Mule"', *Church History* 39, no. 4 (1970), 483–502.

Karkov, Catherine E. (ed.), *Slow Scholarship: Medieval Research and the Neoliberal University*. Cambridge: D. S. Brewer, 2019.

Kidd, Ian James, 'Was Sir William Crookes Epistemically Virtuous?', *Studies in History and Philosophy of Science of the Biological and Biomedical Sciences* 48 (2014), 69–74.

   'Charging Others with Epistemic Vice', *The Monist* 99, no. 2 (2016), 181–97.

   'Confidence, Humility, and Hubris in Victorian Scientific Naturalism', in Van Dongen and Paul, *Epistemic Virtues*, 11–25.

Kintzinger, Marion, *Chronos und Historia: Studien zur Titelblattikonographie historiographischer Werke vom 16. bis zum 18. Jahrhundert*. Wiesbaden: Harrassowitz, 1995.

Kirchhoff, Arthur (ed.), *Die akademische Frau: Gutachten hervorragender Universitätsprofessoren, Frauenlehrer und Schriftsteller über die Befähigung der Frau zum wissenschaftlichen Studium und Berufe.* Berlin: Hugo Steinitz, 1897.

Kivistö, Sari, *The Vices of Learning: Morality and Knowledge at Early Modern Universities.* Leiden: Brill, 2014.

Klein, Esther Sunkyung, *Reading Sima Qian from Han to Song: The Father of History in Pre-Modern China.* Leiden: Brill, 2019.

Knechtges, David R. (trans.), *The* Han Shu *Biography of Yang Xiong (53 B.C.– A.D. 18).* Tempe, AZ: Center for Asian Studies, 1982.

Krajewski, Markus, Antonia von Schöning and Mario Wimmer (eds.), *Enzyklopädie der Genauigkeit.* Konstanz: Konstanz University Press, 2021.

Kramer, Richard L. and Ad Maas, 'A Tale of Reviews in Two History of Science Journals', *Studia Historiae Scientiarum* 20 (2021), 755–85.

Lahiri, Shompa, *Indians in Britain: Anglo-Indian Encounters, Race and Identity, 1880–1930.* London: Frank Cass, 2000.

Langlois, Ch.-V., and Ch. Seignobos, *Introduction aux études historiques*, 2nd ed. Paris: Libraire Hachette, 1899.

Lanzoni, Susan, *Empathy: A History.* New Haven, CT: Yale University Press, 2018.

Lehmann, Max, 'Gedächtnisrede auf Ludwig Weiland', in *Nachrichten von der Königl. Gesellschaft der Wissenschaften zu Göttingen* (1895), 78–80.

Lenz, Max, 'Janssen's Geschichte des deutschen Volkes: Eine analytische Kritik', *Historische Zeitschrift* 50 (1883), 231–84.

Leporin, Dorothea Christiane, *Gründliche Untersuchung der Ursachen, die das weibliche Geschlecht vom Studiren abhalten.* Berlin: Johann Andreas Rüdiger, 1742.

Lerner, Gerda, *The Majority Finds Its Past: Placing Women in History.* Oxford: Oxford University Press, 1979.

Liu Xie, *The Literary Mind and the Carving of Dragons: A Study of Thought and Pattern in Chinese Literature*, trans. Vincent Yu-chung Shih. Hong Kong: Chinese University Press, 1983.

Luce, T. J., 'Ancient Views on the Causes of Bias in Historical Writing', *Classical Philology* 84, no. 1 (1989), 16–31.

Mabillon, Jean, *Traité des études monastiques, devisé en trois parties.* Paris: Charles Robustel, 1691.

Mahanti, Subodh, 'A Perspective on Scientific Temper in India', *Journal of Scientific Temper* 1 (2013), 46–62.

Marcks, Erich, 'Hermann Baumgarten (III)', *Beilage zur Allgemeinen Zeitung* (4 October 1893), 2–5.

Marincola, John, *Authority and Tradition in Ancient Historiography.* Cambridge: Cambridge University Press, 1997.

'Plutarch, Herodotus, and the Historian's Character', in Rhiannon Ash, Judith Mossman, and Frances B. Titchener (eds.), *Fame and Infamy: Essays for Christoph Pelling on Characterization in Greek and Roman Biography and Historiography.* Oxford: Oxford University Press, 2015, 83–95.

Marrou, Henri-Irénée, *De la connaissance historique.* Paris: Seuil, 1954.

Mayer, Arno, 'A Letter to Henry Turner', *Radical History Review* 32 (1985), 85–6.

Meeus, Alexander, 'Truth, Method and the Historian's Character: The Epistemic Virtues of Greek and Roman Historians', in Aaron Turner (ed.), *Reconciling Ancient and Modern Philosophies of History.* Berlin: Walter de Gruyter, 2020, 83–122.

Meinecke, Friedrich, *Straßburg, Freiburg, Berlin: 1901–1919: Erinnerungen.* Stuttgart: K. F. Koehler, 1949.

Momigliano, Arnaldo, 'Pagan and Christian Historiography in the Fourth Century A.D.' in Momigliano (ed.), *The Conflict Between Paganism and Christianity in the Fourth Century.* Oxford: Clarendon Press, 1963, 79–99.

Moore, Timothy J., *Artistry and Ideology: Livy's Vocabulary of Virtue.* Frankfurt am Main: Athenäum, 1989.

Murphy, Kathryn and Anita Traninger (eds.), *The Emergence of Impartiality.* Leiden: Brill, 2014.

Mutschler, F.-H., 'Sima Qian and His Western Colleagues: On Possible Categories of Description', *History and Theory* 46, no. 2 (2007), 194–200.

Mütter, Bernd, *Die Geschichtswissenschaft in Münster zwischen Aufklärung und Historismus unter besonderer Berücksichtigung der historischen Disziplin an der Münsterschen Hochschule.* Munster: Asschendorf, 1980.

Negri, Silvia (ed.), *Representations of Humility and the Humble.* Florence: Sismel, 2021.

Neveu, Bruno, *Un historien à l'école de Port-Royal: Sébastien Le Nain de Tillemont, 1637–1698.* The Hague: Martinus Nijhoff, 1966.

Ng, On Cho and Q. Edward Wang, *Mirroring the Past: The Writing and Use of History in Imperial China.* Honolulu: University of Hawai'i Press, 2005.

Nissen, Martin, *Populäre Geschichtsschreibung: Historiker, Verleger und die deutsche Öffentlichkeit (1848–1900).* Cologne: Böhlau, 2009.

N. N., review of Tillemont, *Histoire*, vol. 1, *Le journal des sçavans* (1690), 313–9.

review of Tillemont, *Histoire*, vol. 2, *Le journal des sçavans* (1691), 205–12.

review of Tillemont, *Mémoires*, vol. 1, *Le journal des sçavans* (1693), 205–11.

review of Tillemont, *Mémoires*, vol. 2, *Le journal des sçavans* (1695), 3–9.

review of Tillemont, *Histoire*, vol. 6, *Le journal des sçavans* (1738), 319.

'Georg Waitz: Zum 9. Oktober 1883', *Die Grenzboten* (1883), 118–26.

Nevins, Allan, *The Gateway to History*. New York: D. Appleton-Century, 1938.

Nolan, Mary, 'Clarifying the Issues', *Radical History Review* 32 (1985), 90–2.

Novick, Peter, *That Noble Dream: The 'Objectivity Question' and the American Historical Profession*. Cambridge: Cambridge University Press, 1988.

Nylan, Michael, *The Five 'Confucian' Classics*. New Haven, CT: Yale University Press, 2001.

Ohara, João Rudolfo Munhoz, 'Virtudes epistêmicas na prática do historiador: o caso da sensibilidade histórica na historiografia brasileira (1980–1990)', *História da Historiografia* 9, no. 22 (2016), 170–83.

Paul, Herman, 'Weak Historicism: On Hierarchies of Intellectual Virtues and Goods', *Journal of the Philosophy of History* 6, no. 3 (2012), 369–88.

'The Heroic Study of Records: The Contested Persona of the Archival Historian', *History of the Human Sciences* 26, no. 4 (2013), 67–83.

'What Is a Scholarly Persona? Ten Theses on Virtues, Skills, and Desires', *History and Theory* 53, no. 3 (2014), 348–71.

'Sources of the Self: Scholarly Personae as Repertoires of Scholarly Selfhood', *Low Countries Historical Review* 131, no. 4 (2016), 135–54.

'Virtue Language in Nineteenth-Century Orientalism: A Case Study in Historical Epistemology', *Modern Intellectual History* 14, no. 3 (2017), 689–715.

'The Virtues of a Good Historian in Early Imperial Germany: Georg Waitz's Contested Example', *Modern Intellectual History* 15, no. 3 (2018), 681–709.

(ed.), *How to Be a Historian: Scholarly Personae in Historical Studies, 1800–2000*. Manchester: Manchester University Press, 2019.

'Ranke vs Schlosser: Pairs of Personae in Nineteenth-Century German Historiography', in Paul, *How to Be a Historian*, 36–52.

'A Missing Link in the History of Historiography: Scholarly Personae in the World of Alfred Dove', *History of European Ideas* 45, no. 7 (2019), 1011–28.

'The Whole Man: A Masculine Persona in German Historical Studies', in Kirsti Niskanen and Michael J. Barany (eds.), *Gender, Embodiment and the History of the Scholarly Persona: Incarnations and Contestations*. Basingstoke: Palgrave Macmillan, 2021, 261–86.

Pennock, Robert T. and Michael O'Rourke, 'Developing a Scientific Virtue-Based Approach to Science Ethics Training', *Science and Engineering Ethics* 23 (2017), 243–62.

Preston, Joseph H., 'English Ecclesiastical Historians and the Problem of Bias, 1559–1742', *Journal of the History of Ideas* 32, no. 2 (1971), 203–20.

Quantin, Jean-Louis, 'Reason and Reasonableness in French Ecclesiastical Scholarship', *Huntington Library Quarterly* 74, no. 3 (2011), 401–36.

Roberts, Charlotte, 'The *Memoirs* and Character of the Historian', in Karen O'Brien and Brian Young (eds.), *The Cambridge Companion to Edward Gibbon*. Cambridge: Cambridge University Press, 2018, 203–18.

Roberts, Robert C. and W. Jay Wood, 'Humility and Epistemic Goods', in Michael DePaul and Linda Zagzebski (eds.), *Intellectual Virtue: Perspectives from Ethics and Epistemology*. Oxford: Clarendon Press, 2003, 257–79.

Intellectual Virtues: An Essay in Regulative Epistemology. Oxford: Clarendon Press, 2007.

Rogacz, Dawid, 'The Virtue of a Historian: A Dialogue between Herman Paul and Chinese Theorists of History', *History and Theory* 58, no. 2 (2019), 252–67.

Chinese Philosophy of History: From Ancient Confucianism to the End of the Eighteenth Century. London: Bloomsbury, 2020.

Russell, D. A., *Criticism in Antiquity*. London: Duckworth, 1981.

Saarloos, Léjon, 'The Scholarly Self under Threat: Language of Vice of British Scholarship (1870–1910).' PhD thesis Leiden University, 2021.

Sarkar, Jadunath, 'The Progress of Historical Research in India', *Modern Review* 89 (1951), 35–6.

Satia, Priya, *Time's Monster: How History Makes History*. Cambridge, MA: Belknap Press, 2020.

Schliesser, Eric (ed.), *Empathy: A History*. Oxford: Oxford University Press, 2015.

Schmoller, Gustav, 'Zum Andenken an Albert Naudé', *Forschungen zur Brandenburgischen und Preußischen Geschichte* 9, no. 2 (1897), v–xviii.

Schnicke, Falko, *Die männliche Disziplin: Zur Vergeschlechtlichung der deutschen Geschichtswissenschaft 1780–1900*, Göttingen: Wallstein, 2015.

Schorn, Stefan, 'Biographie und Autobiographie', in Bernhard Zimmermann and Antonios Rengakos (eds.), *Handbuch der griechischen Literatur der Antike*, vol. 2. Munich: C. H. Beck, 2014, 678–733.

Schrag, Zachary M., *The Princeton Guide to Historical Research*. Princeton, NJ: Princeton University Press, 2021.

Schulte Nordholt, Larissa, 'What Is an African Historian? Negotiating Scholarly Personae in UNESCO's *General History of Africa*', in Paul, *How to Be a Historian*, 182–200.

Shafer, Robert Jones (ed.), *A Guide to Historical Method*, rev. ed. Homewood, IL: Dorsey Press, 1974.

Shapin, Steven, *The Scientific Life: A Moral History of a Late Modern Vocation*. Chicago, IL: University of Chicago Press, 2008.

Simonsen, Jane, 'Consuming Time or Making Time? Slow History and General Education', in Stephannie S. Gearhart and Jonathan Chambers (eds.), *Reversing the Cult of Speed in Higher Education: The Slow Movement in the Arts and Humanities*. New York: Routledge, 2018, 196–208.

Smith, Bonnie G., *The Gender of History: Men, Women, and Historical Practice*. Cambridge, MA: Harvard University Press, 1998.

[Smith, George], *The Britons and Saxons Not Converted to Popery*. London: James Bettenham, 1748.

Stern, Alfr[ed], 'Gedächtnisrede auf Leopold von Ranke und Georg Waitz', *Jahrbuch für schweizerische Geschichte* 12 (1887), xi–xxxvi.

Symonds, Richard, *Oxford and Empire: The Last Lost Cause?* rev. ed. Oxford: Clarendon Press, 1991.

Ten Hagen, Sjang, 'Evaluating Knowledge, Evaluating Character: Book Reviewing by American Historians and Physicists (1900–1940).' *History of Humanities* 7, no. 2 (2022), in print.

Tillemont, [Louis-Sebastién] Le Nain de, *Mémoires pour servir à l'histoire ecclésiastique des six premiers siècles*, 16 vols. Paris: Charles Robustel, 1693–1712.

'Réflexions de M. Lenain de Tillemont sur divers sujets de morale', in [Tronchay], *Vie*, pp. 1–380.

Tollebeek, Jo, 'Commemorative Practices in the Humanities around 1900', *Advances in Historical Studies* 4 (2015), 216–31.

Men of Character: The Emergence of the Modern Humanities. Wassenaar: Netherlands Institute for Advanced Study in the Humanities and Social Sciences, 2015.

Tosh, John, *The Pursuit of History: Aims, Methods, and New Directions in the Study of History*, 7th ed. London: Routledge, 2022.

[Tronchay, Michel], *Vie de M. Lenain de Tillemont avec des réflexions sur divers sujets de morale, et quelques lettres de pieté*. Cologne: s. n., 1711.

Valéry, Paul, 'Rapport sur les Prix de Vertu', in Valéry, *Discours*. Paris: N. R. F., 1935, 115–42.

Van Dongen, Jeroen, 'The Epistemic Virtues of a Virtuous Theorist: On Albert Einstein and His Autobiography', in Van Dongen and Paul, *Epistemic Virtues*, 63–77.

Van Dongen, Jeroen and Herman Paul (eds.), *Epistemic Virtues in the Sciences and the Humanities*. Cham: Springer, 2017.

Van Dongen, Jeroen and Herman Paul, 'Introduction: Epistemic Virtues in the Sciences and the Humanities', in Van Dongen and Paul, *Epistemic Virtues*, 1–10.

Vincent, John Martin, *Historical Research: An Outline of Theory and Practice*. New York: Henry Holt and Company, 1911.

Vogel, Walther, 'Dietrich Schäfer (1845–1929): Worte des Gedächtnisses, gesprochen in der gemeinschaftlichen Sitzung des Hansischen Geschichtsvereins und des Vereins für niederdeutsche Sprachforschung in Stendal am 21. Mai 1929', *Hansische Geschichtsblätter* 54 (1929), 1–18.

Waitz, G., 'Deutsche Historiker der Gegenwart: Briefe an den Herausgeber (I)', *Allgemeine Zeitschrift für Geschichte* 5 (1846), 520–35.

'Falsche Richtungen: Schreiben an den Herausgeber', *Historische Zeitschrift* 1 (1859), 17–28.

Die historischen Übungen zu Göttingen: Glückwunschschreiben an Leopold von Ranke zum Tage der Feier seines fünfzigjährigen Doctorjubiläums, 20. Februar 1867. Göttingen: W. Fr. Kaestner, 1867.

'Göttinger Historiker von Köhler bis Dahlmann', in Friedrich Ehrenfeuchter et al., *Göttinger Professoren: Ein Beitrag zur deutschen Cultur- und Literärgeschichte in acht Vorträgen*. Gotha: Andreas Perthes, 1872, 231–60.

Friedrich Christoph Dahlmann: Gedächtnisrede gehalten in der Aula der Universität Kiel am 13. Mai 1885. Kiel: Universitäts-Buchhandlung, 1885.

Ward, Benedicta, *The Venerable Bede*, 2nd ed. New York: Continuum, 2002.

Watson, Burton, *Ssu-ma Ch'ien: Grand Historian of China*. New York: Columbia University Press, 1958.

(trans.), *The Tso chuan: Selections from China's Oldest Narrative History*. New York: Columbia University Press, 1989.

Weiland, Ludwig, *Georg Waitz (geb. 9. October 1813, gest. 24. Mai 1886): Rede gehalten in der öffentlichen Sitzung der K. Gesellschaft der Wissenschaften am 4. Dezember 1886*. Göttingen: Dieterichsche Verlags-Buchhandlung, 1886.

Westgard, Joshua A., 'Bede and the Continent in the Carolingian Age and Beyond', in Scott DeGregorio (ed.), *The Cambridge Companion to Bede*. Cambridge: Cambridge University Press, 2010, 201–15.

White, Hayden V., 'The Burden of History', *History and Theory* 5, no. 2 (1966), 111–34.

Wiater, Nicolas, 'Expertise, "Character" and the "Authority Effect" in the *Early Roman History* of Dionysius of Halicarnassus', in Jason König and Greg Woolf (eds.), *Authority and Expertise in Ancient Scientific Culture*. Cambridge: Cambridge University Press, 231–59.

Wiseman, T. P., 'Lying Historians: Seven Types of Mendacity', in Christopher Gill and T. P. Wiseman (eds.), *Lies and Fiction in the Ancient World*. Exeter: University of Exeter Press, 1993, 122–46.

Woolf, D. R., 'A Feminine Past? Gender, Genre, and Historical Knowledge in England, 1500–1800', *The American Historical Review* 102, no. 3 (1997), 645–79.

Zagzebski, Linda Trinkaus, *Virtues of the Mind: An Inquiry into the Nature of Virtue and the Ethical Foundations of Knowledge*. Cambridge: Cambridge University Press, 1996.

  Exemplarist Moral Theory. Oxford: Oxford University Press, 2007.

Acknowledgements

I would like to thank Daniel Woolf for his encouragement to write this book, Sjang ten Hagen, Kim Hajek, Alexander Meeus, Dawid Rogacz, Alexander Stöger, and Q. Edward Wang for valuable feedback on draft sections, two anonymous reviewers for constructive criticism, and my entire research team at Leiden University for many fruitful discussions over the course of several years. I also gratefully acknowledge generous research funding from the Dutch Research Council (NWO).

Cambridge Elements ☰

Historical Theory and Practice

Daniel Woolf
Queen's University, Ontario

Daniel Woolf is Professor of History at Queen's University, where he served for ten years as Principal and Vice-Chancellor, and has held academic appointments at a number of Canadian universities. He is the author or editor of several books and articles on the history of historical thought and writing, and on early modern British intellectual history, including most recently *A Concise History of History* (Cambridge University Press 2019). He is a Fellow of the Royal Historical Society, the Royal Society of Canada, and the Society of Antiquaries of London. He is married with three adult children.

About the Series
Cambridge Elements in Historical Theory and Practice is a series intended for a wide range of students, scholars, and others whose interests involve engagement with the past. Topics include the theoretical, ethical, and philosophical issues involved in doing history, the interconnections between history and other disciplines and questions of method, and the application of historical knowledge to contemporary global and social issues such as climate change, reconciliation and justice, heritage, and identity politics.

Cambridge Elements ≡

Historical Theory and Practice

Printed in the United States
by Baker & Taylor Publisher Services